Neat Economic Stuff

Volume 1

Lawrence Clark, PhD

Clark Economics

Winter Haven, Florida

Neat Economic Stuff

Published by

Clark Economics.

Winter Haven, Florida

clarkeconomics.com

Many of the designations by manufactures and sellers to distinguish their products are claimed as trademarks. Where those designations appear in this book and the publisher was aware of a trademark claim, the designations have been printed with an initial cap.

Library of Congress Control Number: 2015948449
Clark Economics, Winter Haven, Florida

ISBN-10: 0996628703
ISBN-13: 978-0-9966287-0-9

Dedicated to My Wonderful Family.
You are missed.

Contents

Preface

Lawrence Clark, PhD is an associate professor of economics at Warner University where he teaches economics to undergraduate and graduate students. This book is a compilation of some of his classroom lectures. From them, students have benefited and have gained tremendous understanding and appreciation for economics and the world around them. It is hoped you will too!

Dr. Clark is a principle and an economist at Clark Economics—a world leader in forensic economic research and consulting—where he is an expert witness and economic consultant. Dr. Clark is a court certified expert and a nationally recognized casino gambling expert. Dr. Clark has prepared research and testified on the behalf of casino industry giants. Dr. Clark's research, findings, and opinions have been reported in newspapers, magazines, TV news programs, and radio talk shows throughout the country. His monthly column on economics was featured in the *Business Journal of New Jersey* among others.

Dr. Clark has authored over 100 articles and reports on a wide range of economic topics. He holds a doctorate from Kansas State University: Manhattan, Kansas in economics; Bachelor of Arts degree in economics from Slippery Rock University: Slippery Rock, Pennsylvania. He did his post-doctoral research on a fellowship sponsored by the Northwest College and University Association for Science: Richland, Washington.

The author wishes to thank the fine and competent staff at Warner University's Pontious Learning Resource Center, especially Sherill Harriger and Mary Thoresen.

Lawrence Clark, PhD
Winter Haven, Florida

Chapter 1

Fun Facts about Technology and Innovation

First, there are two concepts introduced: Invention and Innovation. What is the difference? I like to think that an invention is a new idea or process or a solution without a problem. The innovation is the way to use the invention, new idea or find a problem for the solution to fit. That is how I keep them straight. For instance, 1968 a 3M scientist Dr. Spencer Silver, was attempting to develop a super-strong adhesive but instead invented a new glue that was sticky but not too sticky (a low tack, reusable, pressure sensitive glue). It could not hold things together like regular glue. This was the invention. Years later, someone else at 3M applied the glue to the back of small strips of yellow paper that could be pasted or posted on things—and easily removed—to leave written messages or get someone's attention. This was the advent of 3M's Post-It Notes—the innovation. After several false starts, it did not really become successful until 1980.

Back in the early 1980s, IBM decided to enter the personal computer market. It needed someone to write the operating instructions for its computers. IBM offered a flat $50,000 fee to anyone who would do it. Many computer programmers of the day were not interested, except for one young entrepreneur name Bill Gates. He said he would do it for the $50,000 and on the condition that he would own the copyright to the operating code he developed. IBM quickly agreed; they did not see any value in owning the copyright to software. Everyone at the time knew you made your money selling computer hardware, not computer software. The source code he developed was named Microsoft(ware)-DOS or MS-DOS. Now you know the rest of the story.

The internet started in the mid-1960s among some universities and national laboratories. The U.S. Defense Department's Advanced Research Project Agency (ARPA) got involved with it as a way to strengthen the U.S. telecommunication infrastructure. By the end of the 1960s, ARPA had four computers hooked together; by 1971, it had 18. The internet was designed to be a way for national laboratories and leading universities to stay connected in case a nuclear war disrupted communications. It grew and stayed a university and national laboratory tool until the 1990s. One reason was the arcane computer language and commands needed to use it. This changed in the mid-1990s when Netscape developed a user-friendly browser for the internet called Navigator. Then, everyone got involved with the internet.

As you may know, Microsoft was sued, eventually, by everyone for being a monopoly. The suit grew out of an antitrust lawsuit against Microsoft filed by Netscape. Netscape's Navigator had a monopoly on internet browser software with its Navigator browser until Microsoft introduced Internet Explorer (IE). Netscape did not like this. Microsoft was providing competition for Netscape and threatening Netscape's monopoly on internet browsers. It accused Microsoft of providing unfair competition, because Microsoft would bundle or give away its IE when customers purchased Windows 1998. For Netscape, this was clear evidence of Microsoft abusing its monopoly position.

Microsoft argued, that including IE was just an upgrade that customers expected when purchasing an operating system. For instance, in the early days of computing, you would buy a word-processing program; and then, to make things look nice, you would buy a desktop publishing program. Today, word processing has evolved to the point where you get both a word processing and a desktop publishing program when you buy a word processing program. Customers want and expect this now. This was the point Microsoft was making in bundling IE and Windows. As you know, Microsoft lost the anti-trust lawsuit.

What is funny (odd funny) about the whole thing was that Microsoft was being sued initially for antitrust violations for being a monopoly by a monopoly (Netscape), when Microsoft was attempting to provide competition to the monopoly (Netscape), and Microsoft lost.

Back in the late 1970s and early 1980s, consumer electronics were coming on big with the VCR (videocassette recorder) and declining prices. The VCR would allow consumers to make recordings of family and friends, and play them right back without the mess and delays of processing 8 mm or Super 8 home movies/films. Also, consumers could tape televisions shows and watch them later (known as time shifting).

Many people have forgotten this, but the Hollywood's movie and television industry declared all-out war on the VCR. The industry filed many lawsuits against VCR manufactures particularly SONY (***Sony Corp. of America v. Universal City Studios, Inc.***), more popularly referred to as the Betamax Case.

The movie and television studios felt VCRs in the hand of the consumers would kill the profitable re-run market for televisions shows and movies. The television networks would show the movie or show once, and consumers would tape them, be able fast forward through commercials and never have to watch them again on television rendering Hollywood's re-run rights worthless. Hollywood wanted VCRs banned, or at least taxed at the rate $500 per unit ($1,500 in today's dollars) as they were nothing but a tool for piracy. The tax would be used compensate Hollywood' movie and television industry for lost revenues. Initially, the Hollywood studios won in the courts. The case went all the way up to the U.S. Supreme Court, which ruled for consumers (barely by a 5 to 4 vote) and against the movie and television industry for everyone's benefit.

While the industry viewed the VCR as a substitute for their movies and shows, i.e., it would cost them money. The VCR and later the DVD would be proven to be a complement (make them money), providing a new tool for making Hollywood money by opening up new markets by allowing consumers to buy and rent movies. Today many movies that are flops at the box office can still make the studio money by being released on video, or now DVD. This legal loss by Hollywood turned out to be the best and most profitable legal loss suffered by anyone, anywhere.

To this day, many people fail to realize that if one U.S. Supreme Court Justice had voted the other way in the 1980s, there might have not ever been: VCRs, video tapes, DVDs, Blue-ray, Blockbuster, Netflix, YouTube, etc..

Years ago before we had the HD-DVD or Blue-ray wars of the 2000s, deciding what audio visual standard is best for consumer electronics, a similar war took place in the VCR market. There were two competing systems of VCRs: Betamax (SONY—shorter play time, more expensive, better quality) and VHS (JVC Systems—cheaper, longer play time and lower picture quality). Which was the better system? Betamax had a smaller recording tape cassette—about an hour—and much better fidelity. (The Beta format has been used by many television news stations and professionals and only recently has begun to be supplanted by digital or high-definition tape recordings.) VHS had a larger longer playing cassette tape with less fidelity. They were incompatible with one another; you had to pick one. Betamax dominated early in 1975 with about 100% of the market, by 1981 it was just 25%. VHS stared to gain ground because you could watch longer movies and shows. Beta only had an hour of tape. SONY's chairman at the time could not figure out why anyone would want more than an hour worth of tape. The two formats battled it out for years. Guess what industry finally settled the debate?

If you guessed the pornography industry, excuse me, the adult film industry, you would be right. The adult film industry decided to go with the VHS for its longer tapes and less fidelity. Before VCRs, to get your porno fix, you had to rent 8 mm stag films; it was sleazy and cumbersome to get the projector out, set up the screen and turn off all the lights. Option two: go out to a sleazy, crime ridden part of town to a dilapidated and dirty XXX-theater; but, with a video and a VCR, you could watch porn for hours (if you chose VHS) in the comfort of your living room on your television. It made pornography mainstream. Once the adult film industry went with VHS, Betamax died.

There is an economic explanation for why porn leads the way for distributing itself when new media becomes available—its history. Pornography has always been considered on the outside of society, if not downright illegal; so, it is always looking for new media to distribute itself; one where the law has not caught up with the new technology yet. That is why pornography (or what passed for it) was found on/in: early sketches, paintings, films, the early nickelodeons; the first cable T.V. pay per view channels were porn channels; the first video cassette rentals/sales available were porn, found in adult book stores—not Blockbuster (whatever happen to them?). The internet would not be what it is today without the driving force of pornography behind it. It is the adult film industry's basic instinct for survival that drives it toward new media. That is one reason why pornography choses new media to distribute itself faster than less controversial industries and topics.

The HD-DVD (Toshiba) and Blu-ray (Sony) war of the 2000s had the presented the same dilemma to the Hollywood film and television industry as Betamax and VHS did in the 1980s. With the industry split over format, we needed a tiebreaker. When several large porn firms switch exclusively to Blu-ray, in 2008, it was goodbye DVD-HD—a victory for Sony this time.

The adult film industry: making consumers' audiovisual format choices since ...whenever.

Finally, when music CDs (compact disks) first came out in the mid-1980s, the music recording industry was ecstatic, no longer would they have to worry about music piracy. Until CDs came out, the most popular format for distributing music was cassette tapes, and friends would let friends make copies of their music cassette tapes. This was costing the industry billions in lost sales. Now, CD technology would stop this, as it cost hundreds of thousands of dollars to buy the equipment needed to 'burn' CDs. This good feeling would last until the late 1990s.

And then, there's Shawn Fanning, but that is another story for later.

Chapter 2

Gambling 101[1]

Want to make some money? I will bet that you cannot answer correctly the question: How do casinos make their money from gambling? Do they make their money when you win or lose your bet? Before deciding on whether to accept the above proposition bet (a bet made on some kind of unusual event with a unique outcome, e.g., on which object a fly will land on.), take a tip from the fictional character Sky Masterson from Damon Runyon's play *Guys and Dolls*.

When Sky is offered a bet, he, repeats a warning his father told him: "One of these days in your travels a guy is going to come to you and show you a nice brand-new deck of cards on which the seal is not broken, and the guy is going to offer to bet you that he can make the Jack of Spades jump out of the deck and squirt cider in your ear. But son, do not bet this man, for as sure you stand there you are going to wind-up with an earful of cider."[2]

If you were like the other 99.99% of the people in the world, you would have answered that casinos make money when people lose their bet. Right?

Here is cider in your ear. Wrong! This may sound very counter-intuitive but casinos actually make their money when people win their bet.

The casino does this by paying you less than your due, or alternatively, it does not adequately reward you for the risk you are taking while gambling. Ironically, it means that the casino makes a profit every time you win your bet not lose!

The moral of the story: If someone offers to wager that he can beat you at golf using a broom instead of a regulation golf club, you can bet he is a hustler who gets up every morning and practices with a broom. And, he can probably play the game better that way than with a golf club.

The best way to illustrate how casinos make money when you win your bet is by the following example. Suppose you and I start flipping a coin. Each time it comes up head, you pay me a dollar; and, each time it comes up tails I pay you a dollar. If we play this game long enough, neither of us will make much of a profit. The casino knows this too. So, they change the game slightly. What the casino does effectively is that each time a head comes up and you lose, you pay the casino a dollar; but, when a tail comes up—you win—the

---

[1]This chapter is based mostly on chapter 5 of the same name from *Tales from the Bizarre Side: What Really Happens When Casino Gambling Comes to Town written* by me.

[2]Damon Runyon, *Guys and Dolls*, *The Best Plays of 1950-1951*, ed. John Chapman, (New York: Dodd, Mead and Company, 1951), 50-51.

casino pays you just ninety-five cents ($0.95). With this slight change, the longer we play the more money the casino will make. And that is how the house percentage works.

Casino profits take care of themselves as long as you are losing. It is when you are winning that the casino must protect itself. It does so by paying you less than your due. It should be noted, that the casinos are very clever about disguising the house percentage.

Interestingly enough, many people feel that the way casinos make their money is by manipulating the probability of the outcome. That is, in the above example, they require you to use a coin that instead of having a fifty-fifty chance of coming up heads or tails, they have a coin that comes up heads 75% of the time and tails 25% percent of the time. To add insult to injury, they require you to bet on tails most of the time. However, as we just saw, the casino uses a fair coin—a fifty-fifty chance of either heads or tails—but they get ahead of you by paying you less than your due.

Casinos count on people's misconceptions about gambling, statistics and the probability of outcomes to make their money. Casinos expect to profit from the exploitation of probability theory in applied terms. It works. Casinos earn more in one year than all the lady-luck worshipers put together.

Chapter 3

The Lottery

Lotteries date back to biblical times. They have been used for funding schemes, such as, the Jamestown settlement, Harvard College and the Continental Army. They were never very popular in North America until the State of New Jersey introduced lottery machines that allowed players to choose their own numbers. Before this, players usually purchased tickets with preassigned numbers. Allowing players to choose their own numbers takes advantage of a psychological weakness found in humans. What psychologist Ellen Langer, in 1975, dubbed the "illusion of control". The "illusion of control" is when people tend to infer a power over a chance or random outcome that in fact does not exist. For instance, people will think, they have a better chance of winning, if they pick the random numbers, rather than having someone else pick them for them. In short, people feel they can control the event. When people feel they have some control over a chance or random event, they feel that they are more likely to win and will play the game even more. Lottery players, and all gamblers, apply this "illusion of control" even to random outcomes, where it does not exist.

Almost every state has a state lottery with many different types of games. The big money game many states run is a lottery where the object is to pick 6 numbers out a certain number of numbers. A state, such as, Florida, runs a money–giving–away lottery with a 6/53 lottery. The object is to pick 6 out of 53 numbers. If you pick all six winning numbers, you win the jackpot prize; lesser prizes are awarded for matches of five and four out of six numbers. The odds of winning the jackpot prize are just 1 in 22,957,480. Alternatively, playing twice a week, you can expect to win the top prize once in 220,745 years. Other states, such as New York, run a 6/59 lottery where the odds of winning the jackpot are 1 in 45,057,474; or, playing twice a week you can expect to win once every 433,245 years. And when state governments get together, they participate in something called Powerball where the odds of winning the top prize is just 1 in 175,223,510 million; or, playing twice a week, you can expect to win once every 1,684,841 years—give or take several ice ages. In fairness to Powerball, they did take four numbers away from Powerball a while back and shaved about 200,000 years off your wait time—again, give or take an ice age or two.

The reason some states may offer a 6/49 lottery instead of a 6/53 lottery or why they add more balls or numbers is to offer players bigger jackpots. Adding more numbers results in more frequent carryovers[3] and larger lottery revenues for the state. The fact that bigger jackpots are coming at the expense of less frequent winners, poorer odds and longer waiting times is never mentioned. In fact, the state may say they are doing the players a favor by giving them a choice of playing even more of their favorite numbers.

To add insult to injury, state lotteries have a house (state) advantage of between 40% and 60%. In comparison, a "rip-off" casino game like Keno has a house advantage of just 20% or so; and, many other casino games are far more generous. State governments run games of chance that are two to three times more unfair than the worse casino games.

Making things even worse for the players is the technique used to value the top prize. In lotteries, the technique used is undiscounted nominal dollars or the annuity value of prizes. This technique is popular among lottery officials, sports agents and other fundraisers. It makes a modest sum appear large. Imagine a lottery where the top prize is $1.0 million; the winner gets a $1.00 a year for a million years! When you adjust for the fact that a dollar twenty years (30 years with Powerball) into the future is worth a lot less than a dollar today, you will find that the cash value of stated prize is worth around 60% of its announced value before taxes. If someone offered you $600 thousand in cash today or $50,000 for 20 years, you would be indifferent between the two offers. This means lottery officials do not have to set aside the $1.0 million top prize but only about $600 thousand to pay off the top prizewinner; or, purchase an annuity to pay $50,000 over the twenty years. While $50,000 before taxes is a nice chunk of change, you will not be living the lifestyle of the rich and famous with it.

The general ticket process for playing the lottery is one dollar for one number. Given the odds, the true value of all prizes and the state's high profit margins, a fair value of a ticket is about $0.50 based on one winner. Most of the value of a lottery ticket does not come from the jackpot of $1.0 million or more (six out of six numbers), but from the chances of picking up a $100 or so from matching four out of six numbers (a 1 in 1,416 chance of winning in a 6/53 lottery).

The coup de grâce for lottery players is that many of the games, particularly the state's premier game, are all pari-mutuel. This means the all the winning tickets share the prize money. As a player, you have two things to worry about: 1) are your lucky numbers are going to be chosen; and, 2) how many people are you going to have to share the top prize with—most likely quite a few. If you are like many people, you are probably picking numbers based on birthdays or anniversaries or something similar. You feel this yields a unique combination of numbers, because you feel the probability of two people having the same birthday or anniversary is small. Wrong! In a group of just 23 people, there is 50% chance that two people will have the same birthday. In a group of 75 people, the chances

[3]Carryovers occur when no one wins this week's jackpot and it carries over and is added to the following week's jackpot.

are 99.9% that two people will have the same birthday. Given the number of people that play the lottery, the chances are quite good that you will have to share the grand prize with a number of other lucky individuals thereby diluting the value of your prize. Imagine winning the $1.0 million grand prize and having to share it with a million other people!

Many people believe, incorrectly, that lines form at lottery windows because of the larger jackpots. Not exactly. The true reason lines form is that a ticket becomes a bargain. For instance, in a 6/49 lottery, if the top prize is carried over until it reaches $50 million, the value of a lottery ticket soars to about $2.50 based on one winner, yet it is being sold for just a $1.00. A lottery ticket becomes a bargain even when the prize is adjusted for its true value. Since the average value of a lottery ticket is $0.50, if in one week the ticket is worth $2.50; then, in other weeks, the ticket's value is worth far less than its average value of $0.50.

Are there any strategies to make lottery playing a profitable investment? There have been a number of studies done; most are based on the 6/49 lottery. These strategies may or may not be beneficial to you. Briefly, here are the findings.

You can gain an edge by playing the unpopular numbers. Generally, the non-calendar numbers or play the numbers greater than 31. Why? Not that these numbers have a better chance of being drawn; but, if they are chosen, you reduce the chance of having to share your prize with others. The twelve most unpopular numbers are: 32, 29, 10, 30, 40, 39, 48, 12, 42, 41, 38 and 18. Stay away from the number seven (7); it is too popular. By the playing the unpopular numbers, you can gain an advantage of 3% to 27%, depending on the number. The pitfall of the strategy is that the advantage you gain is very small for the odds you face; therefore, you will most likely fall victim to "gambler's ruin". "Gambler's ruin" occurs when you have a profitable strategy; but you do not have enough income to wait out the time it takes for the strategy to generate enough hits (wins) for the strategy to make a profit. The result is you will end up bankrupt before the strategy pays for itself.

To overcome "gambler's ruin", you could form a dynasty or gambling pool, so that each member buys only a fraction of a lottery ticket. This allows each member's income to go farther, allowing each member to play long enough to generate enough hits for the strategy to pay for itself. Unfortunately, most likely, the original members of this dynasty will be long gone before the strategy works, although their distance heirs could realize profits from this strategy.

Another strategy is to play the numbers that were recently chosen in a previous week's drawing. In studies of pick-3 or pick-4 games, betting on the numbers that won in the previous week falls sharply after the numbers are drawn and only gradually returns (months later) to their former level.[4] This is the belief that lighting does not strike twice. Lottery players feel that numbers

[4] Jonathan Guryan and Melissa S. Kearney, "Gambling at Lucky Stores: Empirical Evidence from State Lottery Sales." *American Economic Review* 98.1 (2008): 458

have a memory, and say, "Well, I was drawn last week, so I better wait a few years before being drawn again." Numbers do not have a memory, and in a fair game of chance the numbers that came up last week, have the same chance of coming up this week. The reason you may gain an advantage by playing them is that many people will not play them. If they do not, the odds are better of you not having to share your prize with others. By the way, the converse of this is also not true: playing the numbers that have not been drawn in while because the numbers will feel guilty about this and elect have themselves drawn this week or next. It does not happen!

Another odd fact about lottery players is that lottery players have a belief in a "lucky store", or in contrast to the above, "lightning does strike twice." When it is announced that a store has sold a winning ticket, the store experiences a 12 to 38% increase in game specific sales in the following weeks, even when other factors are accounted for and controlled[5]. Lottery players do not believe the same numbers will be drawn in a lottery the following week; but, lottery players do believe the same store will sell a winning jackpot ticket the following week. Or, lightning does not strike twice, but yes it does. This is why people feel lottery players and gamblers are such odd fish.

Are there any guaranteed lottery strategies that work? Well, here is one strategy that is theoretically guaranteed to work with a lottery, but technically and practically is fraught with difficulties. It is called "stealing the pot". It takes advantage of the carry over in lotteries. If the lottery jackpot grows sufficiently large, it may pay to steal the lottery or purchase all the numbers. This requires several conditions to occur for this to work: 1) very large jackpots; 2) not many players—in order to reduce the risk of having an idiot savant purchase a winning ticket; and 3) no one else having the same idea. These conditions are usually not met with most state lotteries. Plus, you are going to need a lots of money and a well-run, organized, accurate organization. Because someone will have to go through all 23 million tickets in a 6/53 lottery looking for the 6 out 6 winner; all the 5 out of 6 winners and all the 4 out 6 winners and not miss any. And, you will need the cooperation of lottery sellers who will process your bulk sales (perhaps by putting an out-of-order sign on the lottery machine, while they quietly process your bulk orders in the back office). Furthermore, in a 6/53, lottery you are going to have to spend $22,957,480 at a $1.00 per ticket to buy up <u>all</u> combinations of numbers. Of course, you have only two or three days between drawings to purchase that many tickets. The total value of all the prizes (the 6 out of 6; the 5 out of 6 and the 4 out of 6 winners) will only be about half of the amount you spent or about $11.5 million, with the state's mark up and take; so, you have to wait for several carry overs to occur; and, then move quickly but accurately. If you think that is difficult, think about what would be required to steal the Powerball—at $2.00 per ticket and number.

---

[5] Ibid.

To satisfy your curiosity, it does work. Back in early 1992, an Australian investment group stole the Virginia lottery. Why Virginia? The State's $27 million jackpot had rolled over for several weeks and was the largest in the country at the time. More importantly, Virginia had 6/44 lottery at the time, meaning there were only 7,059,052 numbers to play; so, for a little over $7.0 million investment, the syndicate in less than 48 hours could get themselves $27 million. Not a bad deal. It worked, but the group ended getting lucky as they could not buy up all the numbers as planned; but, they ended up with most of the numbers—about 5 million out of the 7 million possible—which allowed the strategy to be profitable. Outside of this example, everyone else will have to settle for stealing a smaller lottery, perhaps run by a church, school or local charity where the odds and logistics are more manageable.

One final thought. You pay $1.00 for a ticket that has an average value of just $0.50, so why do you pay the extra $0.50? You pay the extra $0.50 for the privilege of having a fantasy. Probably not a bad deal.

Chapter 4

Income Taxes

Did you know it was unconstitutional for the United States to have an income tax? The Federal Government tried to introduce an income tax several times; but, it was always found to be unconstitutional.

As the U.S. Constitution Article I says *"No capitation, or other direct, Tax shall be laid, unless in Proportion to the Census or Enumeration herein before directed to be taken."*

This practically meant no income tax, until the 16th Amendment was passed *(1913)*, which reads: "*the Congress shall have power to lay and collect taxes on incomes, from whatever source derived, without apportionment amoung the several States, and without regard to any cenus or enumeration.*"

The passage of the 16th Amendment to the U.S. constitution in 1913 allowed the U.S. Congress to authorize an income tax.

It is not easy to amend the U.S. Constitution. It requires passage of an amendment by the U.S House and Senate by a two thirds super majority, and must be ratified by three fourths of the States' legislatures.

So, why did the people of the U.S. and the States vote to impose an income tax? It was sold to them as a tax reduction. To get something very unpopular or even stupid passed in U.S. Congress and signed into law by the President, you give the bill a title that has nothing to do with either its contents or its intended effects. For instance, if you wanted to pass a bill to fund a highway to the moon, you would call it: THE PROTECT THE CHILDERN FROM SEXUAL EXPLOITATION ACT; no politician would dare vote against it; and, you will end up with a well-funded highway-to-the-moon project.

Getting back to our story, the people were told that by imposing an income tax on themselves, other federal taxes could be eliminated. Plus, the income tax would be levied just on the rich; and, even then, it would be just a few pennies on the dollar. The entire Federal Government could be financed by having just a few rich people, mostly in the Northeastern United States give just a few dollars of their income to the Federal Government. What could be better and fairer than that? And that is how it was done.

In the beginning 1913, the marginal tax rates (MTR)[6] ranged from 1% to 7%. In 2015 inflation-adjusted dollars, the 1% MTR went from $0.00 to $478,000 of annual income; and, you did not hit the top MTR of 7% until your

[6] The marginal tax rate is the change in one's taxes divided by the change in one's income. It is the tax rate expressed as a percentage applied on the next or last dollar of income you earn.

income exceed at $11,950,000—not that bad by today's MTRs and income brackets. However, these rates did not last long. By 1919, the MTRs ranged from 4%, if your income was under $54,720 to a MTR of 73%, if your income exceeded $13,680,000, again in 2015 dollars. During World War II, the MTR rose to 92% on top income. What happened?

The rich did not have as much money as we thought; and, given that the Federal Government has so many unmet needs, we needed the extra cash. Today the nominal MTRs range from 10%—39.6% with the top rate for single people kicking in at $400,000. The effective MTRs are even higher; because, as your income rises, the deductions you are allowed to take start to phase out, boosting your MTR. If you want more information and the historical tax rates check out the Tax Foundation (www.taxfoundation.org). This is where the above information came from.

While the rich pay a substantial amount of the U.S. tax bill, taxing the rich even more will not solve the Federal Deficit or its spending problem. Using IRS data for tax year 2012 (the most current as of this writing), the "rich", people making over $1.0 million dollars a year make up just 2.5% of all taxpayers, but pay 26% of all income taxes. The "poor" those making less than $75,000 per year make up 75% of taxpayers, but pay just 22% of all income taxes.

For instance, I have estimated that declaring war on those making more than a $1 million a year in the U.S. and confiscating all their adjusted gross income over $1.0 million (a 100% MTR at $1.0 million and above) would yield just a onetime gain of a little less than $1.0 trillion to the Federal Government, enough to cover the Federal Deficit for one or two years—maybe, or fund the Federal Government for three months—both onetime only.

Okay, let's try confiscating all income from those making $75,000 per year or more. No one needs more than $75,000 per year to live comfortably. This would yield an impressive take for the Federal Government of about $3.7 trillion. Now we are talking. This would fund the Federal Government for about one year—maybe, onetime only.

These draconian tax policies would work at most just once; you could not do it again. Why? Because: 1) once you take their money, they will not have it for you to tax again; 2) people will get smart and not earn that much for you take. They will stop earning income a dollar below where the 100% MTR kicks in ($1.0 million or $75,000 income level depending on the tax structure), and then, go on vacation for the rest of the year; or, 3) people will get smart and leave the country and or 4) go underground—as in the underground economy.

In sum, the Federal Government spends money faster than its citizens, at all income levels, can earn it.

Chapter 5

Federal Government Spending

Regardless of what you hear on TV and elsewhere, there is never a cut in government spending. Each year there is an increase in government spending, and it grows bigger each year. Why? Each fiscal year (FY) (October-September) every government agency, department, and program gets a 4% to 10% automatic increase in their budget. The amount depends on inflation and forecasts of program participation and other factors. This is called baseline budgeting, and its purpose is to build automatic spending and tax increases into the Federal Government's budget. If government bureaucrats and politicians decide to reduce the rate of the automatic increase, it is considered a cut in federal spending. For instance, if a department was projected to get **an increase** of $100 billion in spending this year, but gets **an increase** of just $75 billion. They would state, "Our budget was slashed by $25 billion. Children will starve." To make matters worse, the "savings" are projected or carried out over a ten-year planning period; so, this $25 billion reduction in the increase would be announced as a $250 billion ($25 billion times 10 years) cut in federal spending. (Now everybody will starve.) But, it is actually a $750 billion increase in government spending over ten years. If you **froze** government spending at current 2015 FY levels, it would be calculated as a $2.4 trillion plus cut in Federal Government spending over ten years.

Making this more insidious is the fact that this works with taxes as well. If taxes are projected to grow by $100 billion this year and the President and Congress only let them increase by $50 billion, they would announce this tax increase as a $50 billion tax cut! So welcome to the wacky world of government accounting. Politicians love baseline budgeting. They can say they cut government spending and taxes while really growing government spending and raising taxes.

If the Federal Government ran a diet weight loss program, it would be completely worthless but extremely popular. It would be the only weight loss program where you could gain weight, and it would be counted as a weight loss as long as you gained less weight than you thought you did. For instance, if you thought you had gained 10 pounds this week, but gained just 5 pounds. Great job! You lost 5 pounds, at least according to the wacky world of government accounting.

Another little trick politicians use is to agree to raise taxes today and promise that they will really, really cut government spending tomorrow (next year); let's say in the year 2019. Honest, the President and Congress have agreed and sign into law a bill that raises taxes today and forces the next

President and Congress to really, really slash government spending by trillions of dollars tomorrow. Fat chance. One President and Congress cannot impose spending reductions on another President and Congress. Future Presidents and Congresses are free to and will just ignore them. How about those tax increases? They are here to stay.

How could you fix this problem? Have the Federal Government go use zero-base budgeting. This is where every program, department, and agency starts with zero dollars in their account at the beginning of each fiscal year, and every dollar they get to spend must be added to their budget and justified. This would get rid of many federal departments, agencies, and programs that have outlived their usefulness but still exist and get automatic funding increases each year. Spending and tax cuts would have to be real. Again, fat chance of this happening.

Chapter 6

The FAQs of Government Spending, Deficits & Debts

While we are on government topic, to complete the picture, you will need some insight into the federal deficit and the national debt and the implications of such things. While the numbers will change from year to year, the analysis will not. For fiscal year 2015 (October 2014 to September 2015), it is projected that Federal Government spending will be $3,759 billion or $3.8 trillion (remember a 1000 billion=1 trillion); revenues will be $3,176 billion or $3.2 trillion; yielding a deficit of $583 billion (revenues are less than expenditures; or revenues minus expenditures; it is useful to ignore the minus sign).

How does the government spend more than its income? Easy. It charges it or borrows it. By selling government debt instruments called U.S. Treasury Bills, Notes, or Bonds. It borrows the money from a period of several months to about 30 years; and, it pays interest on the money it borrows to the holders of such U.S. Treasury debt instruments. Every time the government borrows money, it adds to the government's liabilities and the national debt; so, if the government keeps running deficits year after year, the national debt will grow bigger and bigger—and it does. If the government ran surpluses (when revenues are greater than expenditures), it would reduce the deficit; if Congress did not decide to spend the surplus on some new or existing need—which it usually does!

In mid-2015, the total outstanding national debt is about $18,152 billion or $18.2 trillion; the amount held by the public is about $13,506 billion or $13.5 trillion. What's the difference? A little less than $5.0 trillion of the national debt is owed by the U.S. Government to itself. In effect, the government is borrowing and lending money to itself. (You do not want to know the how and why of this.) The rest is owned by non-U.S. Government entities such as American businesses and citizens, non-Federal Governments and foreigners. Now that we have the preliminaries down, let's see what are the consequences of all of that government spending, deficits and debts.

The true burden of government spending on society comes from the fact that when the government spends a dollar to do something; something else does not happen in the economy; so, every dollar spent imposes an opportunity cost on the economy. Government spending transfers resources from their highest and best use to usually their lowest and worst use. For instance, the 2009 stimulus bill allocated $80 billion in subsidies (mostly loans, grants and tax credits) to politically connected, mostly green energy companies a number of which have gone out of business and/or have declared bankruptcy. The world famous Solyndra (a solar panel manufacturer) failure and bankruptcy will cost taxpayers about $850 million in loan guarantees and tax credits alone. A lot of useful and productive non-government economic investment activity could have happened with that $80 billion, but it won't. The money is gone forever.

Turning our attention to the deficit, when government runs a deficit, it enters the domestic and international capital markets to borrow money. Since the government is going to borrow the money regardless of the cost of those funds, its action has the effect of pushing or crowding out private sector investment, which must compete with the government for funds. This happens when the government finances the deficit by selling its associated U.S. Treasury debt instruments—Bills, Notes and Bonds. Using bonds as representative of all debt instruments, selling bonds lowers bond prices and causes interest rates to rise. Since businesses borrow money to make money, the higher the interest rates businesses face means fewer opportunities to borrow money profitably, so they do not. This means slower economic growth in the future as private sector investment in new plant, machines, equipment, and research development etc. falters.

For the short term, deficits mean a decline in economic activity because investment is a component of the U.S. Gross Domestic Product (GDP). If investment goes down, so does GDP. Sometimes the Federal Reserve Bank (henceforth known as the FED) has to step in to increase the money supply to prevent interest rates from rising and/or to lower interest rates. This action comes with a cost. It could mean higher inflation down the road, and inflation brings its own set of problems to the economy. Also, the FED may decide it is better for the economy for the FED not to accommodate the increased demand for loanable funds, and let interest rates rise and private sector investment to get "choked off". These are the main short-term problems of running a deficit.

Long-term problems start with the fact that deficits add to the national debt. Is the national debt a problem? This is where a whole bunch of confusion and misinformation comes into the discussion. Initially the confusion comes from comparing the country's debt problem to that of a family. Many people have heard, "Just like a family cannot continuously spend more money than it makes neither can the government." This analogy is wrong on several counts.

First the county is an ongoing concern. It has, theoretically, perpetual life. There is not a day of reckoning for it. The family has a finite life; there will be a day when the family bread winner dies and a final accounting and settling up of the person's assets and debts takes place. Not so with the government. Debt repayment can continuously be put off indefinitely. This is how the government stays in business by running large deficits. Once a government bond becomes due or a payable, it just borrows some new money to pay off the old debt. It borrows the money by selling a new bond and gives the proceeds to bondholder whose bond is coming due. It does this day after day, year after year. It would be like a person using their MasterCard to pay their Visa bill, then the next month using Visa to pay off their MasterCard bill and so on. It works for the U.S. Government because it does not have a credit limit (more on this later) and it has perpetual life—no final day of reckoning. It won't work for an individual for the same reasons—a credit limit and a limited life.

One reason the U.S. Government has no credit limit (unless one is imposed by the U.S. Congress) is the size of the U.S. economy, which can be thought of as the government's income, since it has the constitutional authority to tax as much of the economy as it wants to. The U.S. economy in 2015 as measured by GDP is around $17,985 billion or $18.0 trillion dollars. Since the government can always refinance the principal portion of its debt, the government just has to stay current with the interest payments. This is easy for the government. In FY 2015, the Federal Government has to come up with just the interest payments, which amounted to $229 billion in FY 2015, or at most $20 billion per month. The interest payments are just 1.3% of GDP or its income. Is your monthly credit card, student loan, car payment and mortgage just 1.3% of your income? The U.S. Government is probably in much better financial shape than you are.

Who owns the U.S. national debt could be a problem. Here is an innocuous example. Let's say the government borrows money from half of its population and spends it on the other half of the population. Now one-half of the country owes the other half money. If the government decides to raise taxes to repay the debt, one-half of the population will be poor and the other half-richer—they are paid back. The overall macroeconomic effect is a wash.

Here is another example to clarify the point. Let's say you have a man and a woman dating each other. The man borrows $100 from the woman. The balance sheet for the man would show he has a $100 debt (liability) from this loan; the woman's balance sheet would show an asset of $100 from the loan. Now, they merge or get married. The combine balance sheet for the newly married couple would cancel out the asset and debt. His $100 debt would offset her $100 asset. Their overall financial health is unchanged.

My last example of this event is you get rob of $100 while on your way to buy some party supplies. A theft takes your money and buys some booze with it; the overall macroeconomic effect will be and is the same. It makes no difference who spends the money—you or the thief.

How about the argument that we are passing this debt burden on to our children and our children's children? So what is new about this? Every generation has pretty much pushed current government spending on to future generations. Is this unfair or wrong or something? No. Future generations are benefiting from current government spending. For instance, some current spending could be labeled an investment in human capital as the children are being educated with it. An investment in human capital—education, if done wisely, will allow the children to be more productive in the work force. Higher productivity means higher incomes; so, they will benefit nicely from it, and they will be in a better position to repay the debt.

For those who still concerned about the ramifications of this, think back to WW II. The U.S. financed WW II by selling bonds, pushing some of the cost on to the children and their children. Even today, some of the WW II debt is floating around somewhere having been refinanced a number of times over and over again. Do you not think these children and their children, i.e., you, benefited from having their (your) grandparents fighting and winning WW II? So shouldn't they (you) be expected to pay for some of it? By the way, the people who lived during the WW II years paid a lot more for the war than you may think. They suffered a very repressed standard of living as much of the country's resources were diverted from civilian goods and services production to war goods and services production. They suffered chronic shortages of food, clothing, fuel, automobiles, entertainment etc.. Wars impose a heavy opportunity cost on society.

How about if foreigners own our debt? Now that does make a difference. It would eventually mean a transfer of purchasing power from the U.S. to foreigners. In short run, it would mean we would have more money to spend today; however, in the future we would have less money to spend, as we would have to pay back the money we borrowed with interest. However, this effect is overblown; because, initially foreigners gave us a loan and we had more money to spend, now when we pay the back the loan we will be a little bit poorer as our income is reduced after we pay back the loan. Note: If we invested the borrowed money wisely, we may come out ahead in the deal!

Currently foreigners own about 34% of our national debt. For instance, the two biggest owners of our national debt are China at around $1.3 trillion and Japan at around $1.2 trillion. It is funny that people unusually talk about China, but not Japan when discussing what countries own our debt.

Now here is where people get concerned, needlessly. People assume that China is buying up our national debt to bail out the U.S and to keep us a float. No. China is buying U.S. debt for itself; it has no other place to put all those U.S. dollars it has. It needs a safe, secure place to store its dollars with a chance to earn some interest.

China got all those dollars to buy some U.S Treasury Securities from its chronic international trade surpluses with U.S. in international trade. Since China is selling the U.S. more goods and services than it is buying from the U.S., the U.S. has to make up the difference with cash—U.S. dollars. Since U.S. dollars can only really be spent in the U.S., China keeps the dollars in the U.S. It buys U.S. Treasury securities, because they pay interest and have been historically very safe and are marketable worldwide. They do, however, represent a future claim on the U.S. economy for goods and services. But, since the Chinese basically extended us credit for past purchases of Chinese goods and services, which we have taken but not have fully paid for yet, there is nothing wrong with the Chinese wanting to get paid back. In sum, the

Chinese and Japanese have been large accumulators of U.S. dollars and buy U.S. debt because they need a safe and profitable place to store their U.S. dollars until they spend them or trade them, not because they like us or are doing us a favor.

Okay, how about if the Chinese demand full payment of the debt immediately, would not this cause a problem for us? No. The debt instruments are legal instruments. They have a maturity date, when the principal payment is due. Thirty year bonds bought in 2015 will be payable in the year 2045 not before.

Okay, how about if the Chinese threaten to dump all their U.S. Bonds on the international market depressing their value. The answer is good luck with that. Before they could sell $1.3 trillion worth of bonds, they would have to find a buyer with $1.3 trillion who would want to buy $1.3 trillion of U.S. Bonds. Not too many people or countries have $1.3 trillion laying around waiting for a buying opportunity. Remember: you cannot sell something until someone buys it. If you cannot find a buyer for your item, then you are stuck with it. Moreover, the Chinese would have to proceed slowly in selling in order not to substantially depress the value of the bonds in their rush to sell. There are not too many countries that could afford to lose $1.3 trillion and be around to talk about it. If the Chinese sold all the bonds regardless of price to, let's say, Belgium, it would not change the original legal terms of the U.S. debt instruments to Americans. It would have no economic impact if we send the same amount of money to Belgium instead of China.

Also, you have to remember all these U.S. Government Bonds, Bills and Notes while backed by the full faith and credit of the U.S. Government are not secured by anything. If things ever got really nasty between the U.S. and China, the U.S. could default and say we are not paying off on them. What are you going to do about it? The answer is not much. The Chinese would not be able to "repo" Mt. Rushmore or foreclose on the Grand Canyon. They would be stuck with a bunch of worthless paper. At worse, the U.S. would be another one of the many deadbeat countries, people, and businesses that occupy the planet. I rather be the U.S. than China in this situation owing $1.3 trillion rather being owed $1.3 trillion.

Here is a plan, if you want to pay off the national debt quickly and easily. Have the Federal Reserve Bank (the FED) monetize our national debt. This means having the FED buy up all the national debt by paying straight up cash for each outstanding U.S. Treasury Bill, Note and Bond until all $18.1 trillion of debt is retired. The FED could do this overnight if it wanted.

Now where is the FED getting the money to do so? Is it printing money? No that would be too much trouble and unnecessary. It would just put the money in your bank account and your bank's bank checking account by saying it is there and allowing you to withdraw and spend it.

One caveat, if the FED did overnight, it would expand the money supply and create an incredible hyperinflation—more than the world has ever experienced before. Instead, to avoid the previously mentioned hyperinflation problem, the FED could slowly buy up, lets' say, 5% of our national debt each year using this technique with plans to eliminate the debt in 20 years. American and the world would pay for this debt elimination plan through moderately higher rates of inflation (maybe 5% to 7% per year additionally to what normally happens), which can be thought of a debt-relief tax. What do you think?

Finally, if you wanted to stop the Federal Government's Debt from growing any bigger, just stop raising the debt ceiling. There is a credit limit to the national debt; it is called the debt ceiling; it is around $19.0 trillion dollars. Legally, the government cannot have its total borrowing exceed this amount, unless the U.S. Congress votes and the President signs a new higher debt limit into law. Once the limit is reached and it is not raised, the U.S. Treasury cannot legally borrow any more money to finance the deficit. What would happen if the Congress did not raise the debt limit? Not much. The Government would have to operate on a cash basis where spending just equaled its tax revenues. As previously, mentioned for FY 2015, revenues will be $3,176 billion or $3.2 trillion and this is what the government would be spending; instead of the $3,759 billion or $3.8 trillion being spent in FY 2015; there would be no FY 2015 deficit of $583. You would have a balanced federal budget, period. Clean, neat and simple.

If the idea of not raising the debt limit ceiling ever comes up and tries to be to be implemented many politicians along with the media will claim a government default (the government will not make interest and principle payments to bondholders) will occur and the world will end. None of this would happen. The government will still have $3.2 trillion of annual tax revenues to spend or about $313 billion each and every month. It only needs $229 billion each year or less than $20 billion per month to keep the interest payments current; and, current tax revenues provide some 14 times that amount. The existing debt could be just refinanced within current debt limits. There would not be a default, unless the President deliberately tries to engineer a default by making a decision just not to pay U.S. debt holders, which may not be possible constitutionally.

Why don't they just not raise the debt limit? Because no one really wants a balanced federal budget, even political parties, and politicians who say they do. It would eliminate the fun and games of being a politician and the spending someone else's money and societal resources on their own good ideas and wish list.

Chapter 7

Vandalism and the Broken Car

The economy is in a terrible recession, the auto, housing, construction, and real estate industries are all in a free fall. Then an idea comes along. Pay people to throw rocks through their home, apartment or condominium windows[7]. Better yet, we could get the neighborhood kids to do it for free, if we promise not to prosecute them. Once done, this would require homeowner and renters to go out and hire glazers to replace the window(s), creating jobs and reducing the unemployment rate. Since glazers have good paying jobs, it will boost personal income. Also, the increase in demand for glass from glass manufacturers will stimulate many other industries via the multiplier effect, boosting the revenues and the output of other industries and increasing the country's Gross Domestic Product (GDP). Also, we shall require the new glass windows be energy efficient, so it will be good for the environment. To help out the homeowner/victims, the Federal Government will provide a $1,000 vouchers for the purchase of new windows.

A bit too drastic? Not enough stimulus? How about this then. We still have the recession thing, except the idea is:

It is the duty of all good Americans to go to their fine looking and running car; open the hood; remove the oil plug; drain the oil; replace the plug; remove the oil cap; pour in some liquid glass (death juice); replace the cap; start the car; run the engine at 2000 RPM until the engine seizes and stops. (It actually does die a horrible death.) Now you need a new car. No worries! The Federal Government will give you a $4,500 voucher[8] to purchase a new fuel efficient automobile—where the other $20,000 or so you will require to complete the transaction will come from is your problem! The program will be called the "War On Cars" or WOC for short.

The WOC will stimulate the U.S economy and the GDP numbers, increase employment and reduce unemployment, help the domestic automobile industry by boosting their revenues and output and stimulate other manufacturing industries via the multiplier effect. Since automobile workers and a number of associated industries are heavily unionized, there will be many good high paying decent jobs created, raising the income level of the country to record levels. And, since the new jobs will go to the working man and

---

[7] The following glass story is a modify version of the work of French economist Claude Frédéric Bastiat, "That Which Is Seen, and That Which Is Not Seen" Aka as The Broken Window. 1850.

8 Actually, the dealer would get the voucher to be passed on to you.

woman, it will reduce income equality. To help the environment, the new cars shall be required to get better gas mileage.

Sounds crazy, but this is in its essence was the 2009 Car Allowance Rebate System (CARS); or more popularly, it was known as the "Cash for Clunkers" program, which lasted for two months, July and August, during summer of 2009. Believe it or not, this idea was basically started by an economist as a joke or satire to demonstrate the folly of economic ignorance; but, when introduced, it was taken seriously and quickly gained popularity among the auto industry, politicians and other government bureaucrats. It was the new, "Smart Thinking".[9]

Here is why the vandalism/destruction does not help the economy, promote economic prosperity; but does make everyone poorer and worse off. While being applied to the "Cash for Clunkers" program, the following analysis applies equally for wars and natural disasters. There are a number of people who feel wars and natural disasters are good for the economy.

Imagine every time you built a new car (house), you had to destroy one. Would society ever have any more cars or houses? Would our supply or stock of goods and service be increasing? No. This is what was happening with WOC. We increased new automobile production to replace the cars destroyed, but we ended up where we were with the same number of cars but poorer. Even though we spent more resources (money) building new cars, we did not get any improvement in the number of cars available to consumers. Initially, we spent time, money and resources building 677,842 cars the first time and then destroyed them; and then, we spent more time, money and resources building another 677,842 to replace the ones just destroy. Instead of having 1,355,684 cars (2 times 677,842), we have just the same number of cars, after spending twice the money and resources. Do consumers have access to any more cars? No.

Spending resources to build something then destroying it or having it destroyed is not the way to raise the standard of living for your population. This is why wars and natural disasters are not good for the economy and the standard of living. To promote economic prosperity and raise the standard of living for people, the economy must produce more goods and services and add them to the already existing supply or stock of goods and services. The CARS program did just the opposite it destroyed 677,842 cars, so it reduced our supply and stock of goods. It lowered our standard of living and made Americans poorer.

One reason people wrongly conclude that wonton destruction or wars are good for the economy is the way national income statistics are defined, composed, and calculated. These statistics only look at the additions; they do

---

[9] As an economist, it was a WTF moment when I heard that the Federal Government was endorsing, promoting, and financing wonton vandalism as an economic prosperity program.

not subtract out the losses, so they overstate net new economic activity. During wars and natural disasters, GDP and other national income statistics will show a nice increase; however, all the spending and resources are going just to replace stuff lost and on non-consumer goods; and not create net new consumer goods and services. Again in effect, you are paying twice (thrice) for the same item.

Why did they destroy the old cars? If they had left them on the market in fine working condition, the large increase in the supply of used cars from the CARS program would have driven the price of used cars down. Used cars are a substitute and provide competition for new cars. This would have reduced the demand for new cars; and, since the main purpose of CARS was a continued bailout of the automobile manufacturers, they needed to get rid of the competition by destroying them. Destroying cars reduced the supply of used cars driving the price of used cars up, making new cars more price competitive. Also, since the engine of the used cars had to be destroyed and the body crushed, with a few exceptions, it reduced the supply of used car parts, making it more expensive to repair and keep used cars on the road.

While CARS may have been designed to help the auto industry, it was hurting lower income individuals (a number who drive used cars) by raising the price of used cars and making it more expensive to keep used cars working. Oddly, one of the objectives of CARS program was to reduce income inequality, but CARS was increasing income inequality by reducing the standard of living for lower income folks. One economist even called CARS, "I-hate-the-Poor Act of 2009."

Did not CARS stimulate the economy by creating new jobs, particularly the auto industry? No just the opposite. There is the concept of opportunity cost that is very important in economics. It is your highest and best alternative foregone. Or, every time you do something, you cannot be doing something else. Before the WOC, people who had these cars had them for a while, they were probably paid off. They had no car payment. They had money saved. Before the WOC, they had a car and some money. These people had $20,000 or more[10], either saved or available on credit to spend on other things such as, a new home addition; a swimming pool, a boat, a vacation, a new home entertainment center/theater or something else. Now the WOC destroyed their car, and they had to replace it. Before the WOC, people had a car and $20,000. After the WOC, they had a replacement car, but **no** $20,000 in cash or available on credit, no new home addition, no swimming pool, no boat, no vacation, no new home entertainment center/theater, no nothing else. The replacement car cost these consumers a number of other goods and/or services and the same for the economy.

---

[10] This is obvious since the people who purchased a new car, spent far more than the $4,500 voucher they received. The additional cash came from somewhere, savings, and or, a new car loan etc..

While more money is spent in the automobile sector, jobs and revenues up (actually they went down, more on that later), less or no money gets spent in the home improvement, home construction, boat manufacturing industry or any other industries. In these non-automobile industries, revenue, output, jobs and income decline; and, related industries see a further decline in sales, jobs and output from WOC via the multiplier effect. At best, the WOC would be a wash: the automobile industry up; all other industries down.

There were some formal studies done on the CARS program. Briefly, here are some of the findings. The program was initially supposed to cost just $1.0 billion but ending up costing $3.0 billion as the government underestimated the popularity and cost of government sponsored vandalism.[11]

While CARS was supposed to help domestic U.S. automakers, the program actual boosted cars sales and market shares for foreign carmakers—Toyota came out number one with its Toyota Corolla leading the way.

While one of the objectives of CARS was to increase domestic carmakers' revenues, it reduced them by $3 billion dollars as buyers bought smaller and cheaper cars.[12] The government spent $3.0 billion to increase auto sales, only to end up reducing auto sales by $3.0 billion. That seems about right.

The program did not permanently increase the number of automobiles sold for the auto industry. It just time shifted auto sales from late 2009 and early 2010 to the summer months of 2009. In short, higher summer 2009 sales came at the expense of lower fall 2009, winter and spring 2010 sales.[13]

There was no nationwide improvement in employment from the program.[14] Charities suffered a hit as used car donations fell by 7.5%. During the height of the "War On Cars", the country experienced spot shortages of "death juice" (liquid glass). The "death juice" industry saw a nice temporary increase in sales. Overall improvement in fuel efficiency of newly purchased vehicles during CARS, as measured in miles per gallon, increased by an average 0.65 miles per gallon as a result of the program—for whatever good that did.

Here is my idea for next housing led recession. Let's stop the pussy footing around and go big with the vandalism program. Have all Americans, renters and homeowners, burn down their house, condominiums or apartment. It will be called the "War On Housing" or WOH. The Federal Government will give everyone a new housing subsidy voucher of, let's say, $150,000. The WOH will stimulate the economy by having to rebuild these apartments, condominiums, and homes. Housing prices would rebound nicely.

---

[11] Fox News. "Study: 'Cash for Clunkers' an even bigger lemon than thought." FoxNews.com. August 11, 2014. http://www.foxnews.com/politics/2014/08/11/texas-am-study-cas-for-clunkers-even-bigger-lemon-than-thought/ (accessed June 15, 2015).

[12] Ibid.

[13] , Atif Mian and Sufi Amir, "The Effects of Fiscal Stimulus: Evidence from the 2009 'Cash for Clunkers' Program." *NBER Working Paper Series*, September 2010. 10

[14] Ibid.

Construction employment and revenue would explode; the manufacturing sector would wake from its long-term decline as the demand for new for lumber, plumbing supplies, nails, windows etc. explodes. Other industries would have their sales and output rapidly increase via the multiplier effect causing GDP to skyrocket, the same for personal income. Unemployment will go to near zero as massive new jobs are created overnight.

Environmental concerns could be addressed, as the new homes would be required to be environmentally sound and accommodating. Furthermore, new housing would be built only in existing urban areas to reduce the human foot on the country/planet. Of course, new housing might not be ready right away, so you may have to sleep in a tent for a while. Actually, some you may just have to sleep under the stars, with no tents, as we run out of tents. No worries. Consider this your partial environmental penance for the environmental damage you did while living in your pre-WOH home and driving your pre-WOC car. The rural areas and suburbia would be mostly free of human traffic allowing the ecosystem to be restored to its pristine (non-human) state and condition.

Finally, everyone would get the same type of housing based strictly on family size and needs, not income. The end of housing inequality; everyone gets the same size of environmentally friendly home, except those who are more equal and have more needs and need to live a more open less congested part of the country with a bigger and nicer house than others. This will be determined be the new Secretary of, The Department of Housing and Space Allocation.

Chapter 8

Bonus Happiness

Ever wonder why a car salesman, whoops person, asks, "What type of monthly car payment are you looking for?" Or why many jewelry stores do not have prices on their items, particularly engagement rings? The technical answer is they want to extract your consumer surplus.

Consumer surplus (CS) is the difference between the maximum price you will pay for an item and what you actually pay for it. It is the extra happiness you get for buying something at less than the maximum price you would pay for it. For instance, if the most you will pay is $500, and you only pay $300 for it; you get $200 of CS. Did you ever walk into a store expecting to pay $500 for something and when you got to the cash register, you were only charged $300 for it, because it was on sale and you did not know it? That little extra happiness you experienced is the increase in consumer surplus and utility. Conversely, if you go into the store planning to spend no more than $500 for an item; and, the item rings up at the cash register for $500 or $499; you feel "ripped off"; and, you almost refuse to buy it. This means you are paying your maximum (your reservation) price for an item and the store is extracting all your consumer surplus.

As a business, you want to charge each consumer their maximum or their reservation price that they are willing to pay for an item. You want to extract all of CS and turn it into profit. In practice, this hard to do as you would need to be able to read each customer's mind to find the maximum price they would pay; and then, engage in perfect price discrimination (a different price for every customer) and charge each customer their maximum price. Perfect price discrimination can only occur if you, the consumer, tell the business owner what your maximum price is. So never, ever, tell anyone what is the maximum price you are willing to pay for anything. I know, you are saying, "I would never do that." I say, "I bet you do."

Jewelers usually do not have prices on their items, particularly engagement rings. When a newly engaged couple walks in looking for a ring, the jeweler will ask, "What price range did you have in mind?" Now is the jeweler asking this question to be nice and show you rings in your price range? Or, is the jeweler trying to get you to tell him/her how much to charge you for the ring that you like? (Your maximum price.)

How about when looking for a car and the salesperson asks, "What type of monthly car payment are you looking for?" While you may innocently answer that, you want a payment of no more than $300 per month and can give a $2,000 down payment. Innocent, right?

The salesperson is computing that with a $300 monthly payment for 60 months at 3% annual interest rate and a $2,000 down payment, I can charge this person up to $18,700 for a car they want and like. This method indirectly gets at the maximum he/she can charge you. How would you avoid or get out of these traps now that you know about them? How about, just keep your mouth shut.

When selling something, you want to get as much seller or producer surplus as possible. Producer surplus is the difference between the minimum or absolute lowest price (the seller's reservation price) you will sell the item for, and the price you actually sell the item for. In short, the price right before you refuse to sell the item and its actual selling price. Your minimum price might be $300; and, the actual selling price may be $500; so, you receive $200 of seller's or producer surplus. As a seller, you want to maximize seller surplus, so never, ever tell anyone the minimum price you will accept for something before selling.

Yet, did you ever see the TV show *Pawn Stars?* The first thing out of Rick's mouth when someone walks into his pawnshop with something to sell is, "What are you looking to get for it?" Now you should know why he is asking this question. (He wants to extract the producer surplus and turn it into consumer surplus, since he, Rick, is buying the item.) Do you notice how people happily oblige him by answering his question? Rick has another advantage working for him and that is the "terms of trade" The mere fact you are walking into a pawnshop with something to sell means you are desperate for quick cash. Why else are you walking into a pawnshop? If not, why not wait and sell it on *eBay?* You are more interested in selling than he is in buying, so you can bet he extracts a lot of producer surplus.

Ideally, the free market works to maximizes both consumer and producer surplus and make both the consumer and producer happy when trade/exchange is voluntary. After all, no one engages in a transaction with the expectation of making himself or herself worse off. This is the beauty and efficiency of free markets, it automatically maximizes consumer and producer surplus.

Here is a story of how works—most likely an apocryphal one, though. Years ago, Thomas Edison invented a stock ticker tape machine. It printed out and transmitted the most recent price of stocks traded on the stock exchange—a big deal back then. After much negotiation, Edison agreed to sell the machine and its patents to a large stock brokerage firm for $40,000. After the contract was signed and the deal complete, the owners of the firms smiled and told Edison that, they would have been willing to pay as much as $60,000 for the machine. They were implying that they just "ripped Edison off" by $20,000. Edison just smiled back at them and said, "Gee guys, I was willing to sell it to you for $2,000." In the end, everybody was happy and got a better deal than they thought they would. This is how free markets work when exchange and trade is voluntary.

Chapter 9

Price Sensitivity

As a businessperson and consumer, price sensitivity or price elasticity is very important to you. Price elasticity means how much your buying changes when the price changes. For instance, if prices go up by a lot, does the quantity (amount) you buy change by a little or a lot. Or, if prices go up/down by a little, does the quantity (amount) you buy change by a little or a lot? By knowing a person's price elasticity (price sensitivity), a businessperson knows what price to charge them. You always charge a lower price in the more elastic (price sensitive) market, and a higher price in the inelastic (price insensitive) market.

As a consumer, if you want to pay a lower price for something, indicate that you have an elastic demand for the product. If you want to pay a high price for something, indicate that you have an inelastic demand for it. For instance, if you walk into a new car dealership stating, "My car just got totaled; and, I have to have a new car by tomorrow, or I will lose my job." What you are really saying is: "I am an idiot and have an inelastic demand; please charge me a high price." If you want to pay a low price, you say, you are thinking of buying a new car, if the price is right, but are in no hurry—even if the previous statement is true.

As a business person, you want to be able to figure out what a consumer's true elasticity is, so you can get the most money from them. If the consumer is smart, he/she is not going to tell you or maybe even lie to you. Car salespeople are very good at getting you to reveal your true price elasticity and charging you accordingly for it. For instance, you initially indicate that you have an elastic demand for a new car. The salesman plays along and says, "You can have any car on the lot at dealer's cost." You say, "Great. I will take the white one." The salesman, then says, "Oh, I meant to tell you the white one is our special limited edition model; we only have one. I will have to charge you an extra $500 for that one." If you truly have an elastic demand, you will say, "Okay, I will take the blue one instead." But, more likely than not, you have a preference for the white one and will pay extra for it. After all, why did you select it in the first place? Salespeople are very good at getting you to reveal your true price elasticities and making you pay for them.

Another example is tickets for special events. You will see something advertised on TV or the radio, e.g., tickets $25 in advance $40 at the door. Why? The promoter knows people who purchase tickets in advance have an elastic demand. Generally, they do not have a strong desire to see the event and must be enticed to buy tickets with a low price. The person who shows up at the ticket window an hour before the event is stating: "I intend to buy a ticket and see the event." After all, I drove here, parked and scheduled my evening for the event, so charge me a high price (inelastic demand). By the way, ticket scalpers know this too.

Want to save money on a funeral? Then, preplan it! This fact shows how necessity verses luxury comes into play in determining elasticity. If you stop in a funeral home before someone has died and ask about funeral costs, you will save mucho dollars. Why? You do not have to buy a funeral plan right now. It is a luxury for you at the moment—no need. The funeral home knows that if it wants to make a sale, they will have to cut you a good deal—usually about 50% or more off their post need prices. If you wait until someone has died, the funeral home owns you; because you have to do something quickly. It will not be long after the loved one has died that the hospital or medical examiner is calling you asking when you are going to claim whomever. They will gently remind you that they need the space, and they are not in the body storage and disposal business. You have to do something quickly and will not have much time to shop around for the best deal. The funeral home knows this—so high price.

Moving on there is a very sophisticated pricing problem involving elasticity that theme parks, sporting events, cruise ships and others face. Roughly, it is called the two-price problem. A theme park or a sporting event charges a price for admission. If it charges a high price it will make lots of money at the gate, but not many people will go in, so merchandise sales and food sales in the park will suffer. If they charge a low admission price to get in, but high prices for merchandise, food, gate revenue will be low, but merchandise and food sales will be high. The problem theme parks and other events face: Is what are the correct prices to charge for theme park admission, food, and merchandise in order to maximize theme park revenues?

What makes this complicated is that the sales of admission tickets only depend on the theme park price $Q_t = f\{P_t\}$ where Q_t=number of tickets sold or people in the park and P_t is the price of admission. But, the sales of food and merchandise in the theme park or sporting event depend on the price of the food **and** the price of the theme park admission. For instance, $Q_{hd} = f\{P_{hd}, P_t\}$ where Q_{hd}=the number of hot dogs sold, P_{hd} is the price of hot dogs and P_t is the price of theme park admission. But, the reverse is not true; the price of hot dogs does not influence ticket sales for entry into the park. In short, no one states they are not going to Disney, because their hot dog prices are too high. Even if you thought they were, you just would not buy any while there.

So what are the correct prices to attach to hot dogs and theme park admission to maximize theme park revenues? Disney and other theme parks and other events (although Disney is the best at it) employ a number of PhDs. in economics, statistics and marketing to figure this out. They are constantly adjusting their prices and pricing schemes to figure out the correct prices to charge for both admission and of the many items sold in the parks or event in order to maximize revenue. Of course, determining the correct price depends on accurately estimating the price elasticity of those many items, and a lot of price discrimination (more on this in a future edition).

Chapter 10

The Role of Profits and Losses

Profits along with prices are how resources are allocated in a modern economy. Or, how we make sure resources are going to their highest and best use. The highest and best uses of our resources are the ones that satisfy consumer or societal wants. In this regard, profits, or lack thereof, guarantee that this will happen.

A competitive firm will only make a profit if it is producing a product or service consumers want in the amount they want (not too much, not too little) at the lowest possible cost. If all these conditions are met, the firm will be rewarded with a profit, and it will be maximizing its profits. Profits are a way of rewarding people or firms for doing a good job of providing people with the goods and services they want at the lowest possible cost. The firm is making good use of our scarce resources. Profits are a residual the firm is bestowed for doing a good job.

If a firm is suffering losses, it means it is not producing a product or service consumers want in the amount they want at the lowest possible cost. It is being punished for this with a loss. People are sending a message to the firm to knock off its wasteful behavior; society cannot afford this wasteful behavior given our limited resources. So, Mr. Firm change your behavior or sell your business (assets) to a firm that knows what it is doing, i.e., producing goods and services that consumers want at the lowest possible costs.

One of the dumbest things I have heard a person say is that firms/businesses need to stop worrying about profits or should not maximize their profits; or, maybe, firms should have loses imposed on them as a punishment for past profits. Now that you understand under what conditions, profits are produced: a profit will occur if the firm is producing a product or service consumers want in the amount they want (not too much, not too little) at the lowest possible cost.

Therefore, if firm is not to maximize profit or make a profit at all, the firm needs to produce a product or service customers do not want in excessive amounts at very high costs. For instance, Apple Computer should not be producing new and exciting products consumers want such as, iPhones, iPods, and iPads at lowest cost possible and receiving profits as its reward. Instead, Apple Computer should be producing very expensive garbage and suffering large losses. How about very expensive used toilet paper? Is this what you really want?

Ideally, a competitive firm is in long-run equilibrium when the price of the product equals the incremental or marginal cost (MC)[15] of producing another unit of the product. This means the firm is achieving allocative efficiency. When the price is also at the low point of its average total cost (ATC or AC) the firm has productive efficiency. When both of these conditions—allocative and productive efficiency—is achieved, we are said to have economic efficiency. When both allocative and productive efficiency occur simultaneously, the firm is making zero windfall or economic profits, although it is making a normal amount of profits—just enough to keep it doing what it is doing, no more no less. With economic efficiency and zero windfall or economic profits being made, the firm is in long-run equilibrium. From society's point of view, the firm is being told: good job; keep doing what you are doing; no more, no less.

Now, if something happens like a large increase in demand for the firm's product, the firm will see an increase in its price and expand production. It will also see an increase in profits; it will make windfall or economic profits or what I like to call "bonus profits". Times are good for the firm…for a while; because, economic profits are a signal for other firms to enter the market and start producing similar products or services. Economic profit is a signal for resources and firms to flow into this industry and produce more of the product and service. Eventually all this new supply of product and services will cause prices to fall and windfall economic profits to go back to zero.

For instance, when Apple Computer first introduced the iPhone and iPod etc., it made a ton of money and economic profits. They were earned as a reward for innovation. Other firms saw that a lot of money was being made with the product, and said, "We want some too"; so these other firms entered the industry and started to produce iPhone clones. The supply of smart phones increased; and, the prices of smart phone fell and eventually equilibrium was restored.

In the short run, society wants firms to make economic profits. Economic profits are sometimes called by the public or the media as "excessive profits", "windfall profits", "obscene profits" or even "price gouging". This implies that they are unnecessary and maybe society should confiscate them or prevent them from occurring through the use of price controls. But now you know better. Society wants firms to have "windfall profits" as a way of attracting more resources and more firms into an industry that is producing a product consumers want more of, and eventually prices and profits will return to normal levels.

The converse is true of economic losses which are a signal to firms and resources (such as workers) to produce less of a product or service and to leave the industry; and, go to an expanding industry; one that is experiencing economic profits. The higher cost firms will be the first to leave, supply will shrink, and equilibrium and zero economic profits will be restored. From

---

[15] Marginal cost or incremental cost is how total costs change when quantity or output increases by one unit.

society's point of view, the firms in the losing industry are being told: "Knock it off. You are wasting resources; we do not want as much of your product as we did before." This frees up resources for industries that are producing goods and service that consumers or society really want.

Economic loses do not always mean accounting losses. For instance, you may have heard of a family business shutting down or selling out. And, you may inquire, "What happen? Weren't they making any money?" The answer you may hear back is "They were making money (accounting profits); but, they felt that it just wasn't worth it (suffering economic losses)."

You do not want to stop businesses from suffering losses or from going out of business through government programs or subsidies; nor do you want to feel sorry for them or their workers. In fact having firms go out of business and leave an industry is the only way you can stabilize the industry. It is this constant oscillation between economic profits and economic losses—firms going into business, and firms going out business—that help insure that resources are going to their highest and best use. And, that's what happens in a market economy. In a market-oriented system, both profits and losses are equally important in allocating resource to their highest and best use and consumers' wants are being satisfied.

Chapter 11

Money for Nothing—Monopoly

When speaking of monopoly everybody wants to be a monopoly, because there is easy money to be made. But, first what is a monopoly? Monopoly means a single seller of a product or service of which there is no close substitute. A monopoly restricts or curtails output or production of the product or services, has high prices, makes economic profits and does not innovate.

Just because you are a single seller of a product or service does not mean you are a monopoly. For instance, if I lobby the U.S. Congress to grant me an exclusive carrier pigeon franchise in the United States for communication purposes, am I a monopolist? No. While I am a single seller of the service by law, there are many good substitutes for my product such as, email, snail mail, telephone, radio, telegraph, FAX etc.. So, in effect, I have what is called a worthless monopoly (a monopoly that does not make an economic profit; but suffers only losses).

Monopolists make money by restricting output. Or, given the price and resources that they have available to them, do not produce as many goods and services as they could or as a perfect competitor does. In in some situations, a monopoly may produce only half as much output as a perfect competitor does.

A monopolist does not create shortages; the monopolist charges a price high enough to clear the market at that output level. It is not in the interest of the monopolist to create a shortage. If the monopolist did, they would not be benefiting from their monopoly position. In sum, a monopolist produces less output, charges higher prices and makes windfall economic profits in both the long-run and short run (all the time). Why? Because, competitors cannot enter the industry and compete against them. The monopolist is protected by barriers entry.

Most effective barriers to entry are created by the government. These barriers prevent firms from entering the industry and competing against the monopoly, preventing output from increasing, supply from increasing, prices from falling and economic profits falling to zero.

Ideally, many people want to become a monopoly, because you get to make lots of money without having to work hard for it. But, this is difficult to do; because, once you start making money, everybody, including your competitors, wants in on it. Only if there was some way you could prevent competition. I know. I shall lobby my friends in government to prevent competitors from entering the market. Of course, to prevent this from sounding too self-serving, I will announce that it is for some good reason, such as, to promote orderly and stable markets, prevent the wasteful duplication of service and resources, or protect the public safety and convenience. For these reasons, I need to be the only seller of the product or service. These are the reasons given for having one cable TV company in a city, one electric utility, or one hospital serving an area. These reasons sound a lot better than help me make more money at your expense. Don't they?

On the more palatable level, the Federal Government grants monopoly privileges to encourage inventiveness and creativeness; this is done through the granting of patents and copyrights. A copyright is better than a patent. It lasts longer. While it is complicated and depends on many factors, a copyright generally lasts for the life of the author, plus 75 years after their death. That is why the songwriter in a rock band, for instance, makes more money than the other band members. He gets money for playing in the band; plus, the band has to pay him/her royalties for recording and playing his/her song. Of course, he/she can sell the rights to his/her song to another band for lots of money, which has happened. Want to play or record someone else's songs for commercial purposes, then expect to pay lots of money for the right to do. If you do not, expect to be sued for lots of money.

By comparison, a patent generally lasts just 20 years. To get one, you have to apply to the U.S. Patent Office sending along with it all the details of how and why your idea is different and works. All this information makes it easy for someone to "reverse engineer" your invention, make some changes, call it something different, and steal your invention. Of course, you may try to sue for this. But, given all the hassles and short life of a patent, some companies instead maintain trade secrets. They just do not tell anyone what their idea is or show how their idea or invention works. Some famous trade secrets are the formula for Coca Cola syrup, Kentucky Fried Chicken—the Colonel's 11 secret herbs, and spices.

While 20 years sounds like a long time, it is not, especially for drug manufactures. Once the company finds a promising new drug, it takes around ten years of testing and $800 million to bring just one drug to market. Of course, after you spend all this time and money, the U.S. Food Drug Administration (FDA) could still say, "no"; you cannot sell your drug, so you lose all your money as several diet drug companies found out. Assuming everything goes along smoothly, you only have about ten years to recoup your investment and make some money off your invention before the patent expires. Hopefully, the economic profits that are generated by the patent allow the drug company to staff and finance their research division, work on new wonder drugs of the future and cover the costs of all their failures and unapproved drugs.

After your patent expires, your monopoly expires and anyone and everyone can legally steal your drug recipe and start manufacturing it. The market model shifts from monopoly to perfect competition, as the product becomes a homogenous (a generic) product. As firms enter the market and start to producing the drug, supply increases, prices drop to the perfect competition level and economic profits return to zero.

Chapter 12

Oligopoly—Monopoly Lite

Remember monopoly is a single seller of a product of which there is no close substitute. If there is more than one firm, it is not a monopoly. Generally, an oligopoly is an industry with more than one firm and less than 100. When I think of an oligopoly, I think of around four firms. The oil industry and pharmaceutical industries can be described as oligopoly (a few large firms). Briefly, it is monopoly lite. Oligopoly has the second highest prices behind monopoly and the second lowest output levels behind monopoly. There are economic profits, but they are less than those of an unregulated monopoly. There are barriers to enter, but not insurmountable ones. Firms with enough money and capital can enter and compete with existing firms.

While oligopolists do make economic profits in both the long run and short run, it is not necessarily bad as they use those funds to fund research and development, inventions and innovations and to expand production. A firm in perfect competition does not have the money, i.e., economic profits, to start and finance a large research and development division nor to engage in a long, lengthy and expensive drug approval process. It takes an oligopoly with some long run economic profits to do so. That is one reason why economic profits exist.

The pharmaceutical industry is an oligopoly. They do have competitors. They may have a monopoly on (for) a given drug(s) for a short time period. While a firm could produce a new drug to fight diabetes and get a patent on it, other firms could invent new patentable diabetes drugs and sell them to compete with the existing firm.

The oil industry on one level may be described as oligopoly on one level and monopolistic competitor on another (retail gas stations). Notice, I said **monopolistic** <u>not</u> **monopoly**; there is a difference. Any economic profits the oil and gas industry makes are plowed back into production of more oil and natural gas. They spend their profits on exploring, finding and developing new sources of oil and natural gas. This is not cheap. After many promising tracts of land are explored, drilling rights acquired and wells drilled; the property may yield little or no commercially viable amounts of crude oil and natural gas.

While many people were focusing the environmental damage the BP oil spill was allegedly doing in the Gulf of Mexico in 2010, many people failed to look at and appreciate capital investment and technology at work. Over a mile under the sea, there was a full-scale construction, demolition, mining and manufacturing operation occurring which involved drilling some two miles into the earth, using the latest in remote sensing and submersible technology. All to bring you, the least cost oil and natural gas supplies and products. When the oil spill occurred, the U.S, Government, and even the U.S. Navy could not get involved, as they did not have the knowledge, skill set, or the technology the oil companies had in working deep under the sea. The oil companies developed it from years of R&D financed by economic profits.

Chapter 13

How to Form a Cartel

If you cannot be a monopoly, then try to act like one with your competitors by forming a cartel. A cartel allows several firms to operate as a single firm and make more money or economic profits than operating separately. Ideally, there can be only a limited number of firms. The more firms, the more difficult it is to do. That is why oligopolies are the best industrial structure to form a cartel. Here is the rest of the secret formula:

> Have a small number of firms with market power. The fewer the number of firms the better; it is easier to assess how much each firm should restrict production; it is easier to monitor compliance with the cartel's agreement, so there is no cheating.
>
> Have barriers to entry to prevent firms entering the industry and undermining the cartel. Look to the government for help.
>
> Have a relatively undifferentiated products or a homogenous product. If everyone sells the same products, there should be no price difference among cartel members, if everyone is following the agreement. With heterogeneous (different) products prices, a cartel member could argue that its prices reflect quality difference of its superior (inferior) products and not cheating.
>
> Have easily observable prices. If the prices are posted publicly, it is easier to ensure firm compliance with the cartels agreed upon price.
>
> Have little variation in prices on both the input and the output side. This requires a stable demand and supply for both output side and the input side. If prices on either the output side or input side fluctuate a lot, it is more difficult to detect cheating, since the accused firm could just say its costs have changed.
>
> Have a meaningful way to punish cheaters.
>
> Have an inelastic demand and supply curves—especially for non-cartel members. This is so the supply of the output by non-cartel members cannot increase easily in response to the high prices charged by the cartel members. On the demand side get rid of substitutes for your product or service to reduce the price elasticity of your demand. Find a way to have substitute (competitors) products or services experience price increases. Say, "Hello government."
>
> Finally get together with member firms and agree what the market demand is for your product, then calculate the industry's incremental

or marginal revenue(MR)[16] curve along with the industry's cost curves including the MC curve. Equate the MC=MR and charge a price that clears the market at that level of output. Just like a monopolist. In fact, a cartel's structure is one in which a few firms get together and try to act like one firm or a monopoly.

Once the price and joint output are determined, give each firm a share of the output to produce or its quota. This can be the source of much disagreement and the source of much cheating among cartel members. In fact, some firms may be asked not to produce anything or shut down completely, because their costs are much higher than other cartel member's costs are. Of course, these firms must be compensated with a share of the cartel's economic profits, in excess of what the firm could have earned operating independently of the cartel.

Doing all of the above is not easy. All firms have different ideas of what their market demand is, and what their costs are. Therefore, every firm has a different idea of what the profit maximizing price and output should be. For the cartel to be meaningful, it must have the promise of making each member more profits operating as a collective than each would operate independently.

Moreover, some firms are not going to be happy with the cartel's decision on the cartel's joint price and their share of the output. Some firms, of course, will be happy with the cartel's decision because the cartel's decision on price and output are very close to their own profit maximizing price and output levels, if they were operating as monopolist. Generally, these are the larger or dominate firms of the cartel.

With cartels, the incentive to cheat is high. As a producer, if I were told to produce only 50,000 barrels of oil a day while the other cartel members were allowed to produce 100,000 barrels of oil per day. I am going to think I am getting screwed on this deal. I will start to cheat and expand my production to 60,000 or 70,000 barrels per day and sees what happens. Of course, this expanded output puts downward pressure on prices and the cartel will collapse. And, cartels usually do because of cheating. Moreover, the hard times of recessions can cause firms to think even more about cheating on the cartel agreement. Now you should have an idea of why cartels breakdown and do not last long.

Sometimes, if there is a dominant or low cost firm in the cartel, it can punish the cheating member by expanding production so much it pushes the price below the cost of production for the cheater. The cheater will lose money unless he/she changes their ways and abides by the cartel agreement. It is not always successful and just buys time until the cartel collapses. Sometimes Saudi Arabia does this among cheating OPEC members. In another case,

[16] Marginal revenue is the change in total revenue when the firm sells one more unit.

when Kuwait exceeded its OPEC quota and started sending oil prices down in the early 1990s, Iraq just invaded Kuwait and put an end to this cheating. This along with a little slant oil drilling by Kuwait was the root cause of the first Gulf War.

The only way cartels can survive in the long run is with the help of government. For instance, the U.S. Government bestows cartel privileges on three U.S. risk ratings agencies: Fitch, Moody's, and Standard & Poor's. These three firms have been designated Nationally Recognized Statistical Rating Agencies. The Fed and U.S. Securities and Exchange Commission will not accept financial ratings from other rating firms, except for these three. This creates a very high barrier to entry for potential competitors. These three firms take advantage of this de facto government created and sponsored cartel by charging similar fees and assigning identical risk ratings to similar securities—much to determinant of investors. All with the blessings of the U.S. Government.

Some other cartels you may have heard of that have existed with various degrees of success: DeBeers—diamonds; OPEC—oil; NCAA—college sports; various agricultural cartels-—milk, caviar, coffee; minerals, such as, bauxite, copper and mercury. Then, there is the FDA sponsored cigarette cartel. The next chapter gives a detailed breakdown on how the U.S. Government created and maintains the world's largest cigarette cartel.

Chapter 14

The Profitable FDA Sponsored Cigarette Cartel

The mantra of many economically ignorant people especially the "do gooders" and many in the media is: government regulation, good (any regulation); and no government regulation, bad. Many people incorrectly assume that businesses do not want government regulation and consumers do want government regulations to protect them from the ravages of unfretted business exploitation. However, nothing could be any further from the truth.

Businesses actually want to be regulated in order to have their products sold by government mandates imposed on consumers and to be protected from the ravages of unfretted competition and exploitation by demanding consumers, who from some reason want low prices on items and the unfretted freedom not to by a product at all. The one piece of Federal Legislation that definitively demonstrates this is The Family Smoking Prevention and Tobacco Control Act (henceforth referred to as the ACT). This act gave the Food and Drug Administration (FDA) regulatory authority over tobacco products and industry. The ACT was supported (and essentially written) by the cigarette industry—led by Altria (aka Phillip Morris, USA, of Marlboro cigarettes fame).

Some of the relevant economic highlights of the ACT are as follows. The FDA has to approve all new and existing tobacco products, with grandfathering for products available before 2007; essentially end all forms of advertising such as, free samples, sponsorship of sporting/entertainment events; require the listing of all ingredients contained in the product on the label. Outlaw misleading claims and force them to proof claims of "reduce risk" or "reduced exposure" (aka "light", "mild", "low" cigarettes); require strong warnings on smokeless tobacco products; prevent the selling of flavored cigarettes, except for tobacco flavor and menthol; prevent the FDA from outlawing cigarettes and reducing nicotine to zero and prohibit the raising of the smoking age past 18; keep misleading cigarettes or counterfeit tobacco products off the market; require graphic and visual death warnings on tobacco products.[17]

The requirements sound very tough; why would any industry want these regulations? Because what the law did, courtesy of the ACT and FDA, was create a very large profitable and enduring cigarette cartel for the Big Three cigarette/tobacco firms[18]. A cartel that is impervious to extinction, and has the

---

[17] "Family Smoking Prevention and Tobacco Control Act" Pub.L. 111–31, June 2009 H.R. 1256. n.d.

[18] In the U.S. in terms of company market share: 1) Altria Group, Inc., brand Marlboro; 2) Reynolds American, brands, Camel, Pall Mall, and Newport; and 3)

FDA administering and protecting the cartel—a cartel that will allow the larger and established domestic tobacco companies to thrive and prosper. Some of the unintended effects will be that it will increase tobacco prices, put and keep more dangerous smoking products on the market, reduce or eliminate the number safer tobacco/nicotine products on, or coming to the market and increase the number of deaths from smoking—but who cares.

First the FDA and Act are going to make the cigarette manufactures more money by increasing the demand for cigarettes The simple fact that the FDA is in charge of implicitly promoting cigarette use is going to be a positive for the cigarette industry which has long suffered from an imagine problem in the past. For many people, their familiarity with the FDA comes from the FDA's role in approving new drugs for use. They know the FDA approves new drugs only after they have been proven "safe and effective." Remember, the FDA has banned rather innocuous substances such as, Trans Fats; so, if they, thought cigarettes were really bad, they would ban them. Right? Actually, no. They cannot by law.

Now smokers and nonsmokers read this headline, FDA APPROVES 48 NEW CIGARETTE BRANDS. Some of that "safe and effective" will transfer over. People will think other cigarettes are bad, but these approved ones must be the better ones or the lessor of the bad ones. Else, why would the FDA make this announcement, approving only these new cigarettes? They must be the safe ones. It also conveys the impression that if cigarette smoking is a problem in the U.S.A., it is going to get better; and, do not worry; the FDA is in charge and will have the situation fixed in no time.

How is the prohibition of advertising good for the industry? While the anti-smoking groups fixate on advertising as the cause of smoking, something along the lines of, "if we would ban cigarette advertising people would quit and not start and the join the ranks of smokers." This is incorrect. People have been using tobacco for 1000s of years, and the modern smoking era has existed for 100s of years as cigars, pipes and later cigarettes came of age. People were drawn into using and smoking tobacco for its pleasure, stimulation, relaxing and stress reliving properties among many other effects. People started smoking well before cigarette manufactures and their advertising came along. And you know what? They will start and continue to smoke long after cigarette advertising is banned.

The only thing cigarette advertising did was to temporality increase the sales and market share of a particular band or firm, until the other firms and brands responded with their own advertising campaign. For instance, Brand A starts a $10 million ad campaign to steal customers from Brand B; to counter it, Brand B starts its own a $10 million ad campaign to steal the customers back. The end result is Brand A and Brand B will end up with the same market share and sales, but both are $10 million poorer and their combined profits are

---

Imperial Tobacco Group, brands Salem, Kool and Winston.

$20 million lower due to advertising expenditures. Wasteful. It would be in their interest to get together and agree not to engage in expensive and unproductive advertising against each other. This limited cartel would be difficult, but profitable, to do; and illegal under a number of antitrust statutes. Unless of course, the government makes the cigarette industry stop advertising and enforces the advertising ban.

The first ban on cigarette advertising occurred in 1971 when the Federal Government banned cigarette television and radio ads. Its effect was immediate as cigarette industry profits soared by 40%.[19] How did the industry get cigarette ads banned? With a little help from anti-smoking groups and the print and newspaper industry, the latter were the beneficiaries of all these newly freed up advertising dollars. Removing cigarettes ads from TV and radio had another benefit for the cigarette industry. Under the "Fairness Doctrine" of the time for every cigarette ad that was aired, meant equal time had to be provided to an anti-smoking group and their message. No more cigarettes ads on TV and radio meant no more anti-smoking messages. The Fairness Doctrine" did not apply to other media.

The 2009 ban on all advertising has the same profitable effect and more. In addition to boosting profits, by eliminating advertising expenses, it protects the industry from potential competitors and helps maintain and preserve current market shares and the sales of current cartel member brands. For instance, a new brand of cigarettes called "Clarkettes" comes on the market, how are people going to find out about this? How is #3 Camel going to catch #2 in sales Newport or #2 ever going to catch #1 Marlboro cigarettes without a clever and competitive advertising campaign, etc..

Now you may think, "Does not the ACT's requirements that require cigarettes packages to carry large graphic pictorial death warnings going to hurt sales and negate some of the above?" Nope. They are not going to happen. They were put into the law to prevent the ACT from sounding too favorable to the industry. The pictorial death warnings would (and have been) been overturned by the courts on first amendment, commercial speech, grounds.

Further promoting the Big Three's FDA enforced cartel are barriers to entry for potential competitors. New competitors have to have their product approved by the FDA. To win approval, the new brand has to prove that its new brand is sustainably equivalent to a product on the market—to prove it will not add any new health questions. This requires that you choose a competitor's product and provide details for a comparative analysis.

Good luck with this. Submitting a FDA application will take about 5,000 hours and cost about $300,000 for one brand.[20] In fact, one potential new

[19] , James L. Hamilton,"The Demand for Cigarettes: Advertising, the Health Scare, and the Cigarette Advertising Ban", *Review of Economics and Statistics*, 54, no 4 (1972): 401-411.

[20] Sally L. Satel, M.D. "Will the FDA Kill Off E-Cigs." *New York Times*. January 18, 2015. Retrieved from http://nyti.ms/1axlOxp (accessed June 18, 2015).

competitor, Hestia Tobacco, had to argue with the FDA for over a year just to get its brand name, Hestia, approved—never mind getting started on, or having its product actually approved. In the end, the FDA can just say you did not meet the ACT's requirement of specifying a proper predicate (similar) product for your study. Start over. Better yet, the FDA can just ignore the application, and claim there is no time limit on the approval for similar products. What is the new competitor going to do? Not much.

The established major cigarette companies have a number of similar brands to choose from and the detailed comparative analysis already done. Plus, they have experienced in-house research facilities to crank out the needed numbers to keep the FDA satisfied, an experienced in-house legal team to push the approval through the FDA bureaucracy and the legal talent to threaten the FDA with lawsuits should they not approve it. Upstart competitors do not have such in-house endowments.

The next step in maintaining a successful cartel is get rid of non-cartel competitors or price and hassle them to ineffectiveness. This happened with the RYO (Roll Your Own) cigarette industry. They were a number of retail stores that sold bulk tobacco and provided consumers with the use of automated equipment to manufacture their cigarettes. The reason this industry thrived for a while was the personal exemption part of the Internal Revenue Code. For a long time, a one-pound bag of tobacco had only $1.10-pound tax rate placed on it, much less than the tax rate for commercial use. This gave the RYO industry a big advantage over the large cigarette companies and Big Tobacco did not like it, so they attacked it. First, they lobbied to have the tax raised to around $25.00 per pound. This lead to a decrease in the popularity of RYO cigarettes as their price competitiveness diminished. The next step in harassing the RYO came in 2012 with an amendment to a transportation bill. In order for RYO to continue the use of automated cigarette machines operated by their customers, the RYOs had to: obtain a manufactures permit; file a bond; pay the applicable federal cigarette tax; keep records, print required markings; print the surgeons warning; and comply with the FDA's package size. This pretty much killed off the RYO industry and protected Big Tobacco from competition from this industry.

Ever wonder why flavored tobaccos are banned, except menthol and tobacco flavors? The anti-smoking groups will say it is to protect the youth from thinking cigarettes are candy-like. Nope. Menthol and tobacco flavored cigarettes are mostly manufactured domestically in the U.S. by the Big Three cigarette manufactures. Other flavors are mostly manufactured by foreign competitors. It is an attempt to keep foreign cigarettes out of the U.S. further protecting the FDA's cigarette cartel—allegedly on health and safety grounds—without openly violating and international trade agreements. This last part could be in trouble. Indonesia successfully filed a complaint against the U.S. with World Trade Organization (WTO) claiming that this flavored cigarette ban was in violation of various trade agreements. Indonesia won.

Whether this has any effect on the U.S. cigarette market with the flavored tobacco ban has yet been determined.

Some people feel smokeless tobacco may be a safer alternative to cigarette smoking and switch over to this other form of tobacco use to reduce the health risk from smoking tobacco. The ACT, the FDA and the tobacco industry is going to try to discourage you from thinking smokeless tobacco is a good substitute for good old cigarette smoking by misrepresenting the risk from smokeless products. Smokeless products have to carry a self-serving warning, courtesy of the cigarette industry, in large types: "**Warning: This product is not a safe alternative to smoking.**" However, "a vast majority of scientific evidence suggests that smokeless tobacco is substantially safer than smoking."[21] Britain's Royal College of Physicians in 2002 described smokeless tobacco as between 10 and 1000 times less hazardous than smoking…."[22] Unfortunately, Americans are kept in the dark about these risk reduction facts, because it is not in the industry's nor the anti-tobacco/smoking group's interests to do so. Another study shows that cigarettes kill 50% of addicted addicts and up to 63,000 Americans nonsmokers (second hand smoke effects, if you believe it), but smokeless tobacco kills about 1% of its addicted uses and ZERO non users[23]. Much better. But, they cannot tell anyone about this. In fact, they have to state just the opposite.

The FDA, according to the ACT, must remove counterfeit and bootlegged cigarettes from the market, which are substitutes for genuine cigarettes. What industry would not want to have a multi-billion-dollar federal agency policing the marketplace for them and removing counterfeit products for them, so they do not have to spend their own money doing so. This has an effect on the cost side and revenue side for the industry. You can bet the Recording Industry Association of America (RIAA) is envious and wish they had a dedicated billion-dollar federal agency getting rid of P2P websites for them.

Modified Risk cigarettes (the ones that were labeled "low tar", "mild" "light") had this descriptor removed from the labels. Yet, they could maintain other unique identifiers of their brand and packaging. For instance, Marlboro Lights have always come in a distinct white and gold colored box. A customer in the past would ask for Marlboro Lights. Today the customer would just ask for Marlboro Gold. It is the same product with a "special blend" of tobacco for that "smooth flavor"—just different words.

---

[21]Charles Capella, R. Taylor and Michael L. "Smokeless Tobacco Products as a Harm Reduction Mechanism: A Research Agenda." *Journal of Public Policy & Marketing*, Fall 2008: 188.

[22] Ibid. p. 189.

[23] William T. Godshall, MPH. E-Cigarettes Politics. September 20, 2004. http://www.ecigarette-politics.com/fda-approves-44-cigarette-brands.html (accessed June 25, 2015).

Everyone knows that it is difficult for smokers to quit smoking completely, according to a National Institutes of Health report only 5% of smokers quit each year.[24] What the cigarette industry is more worried about is smokers switching to safer tobacco cigarettes, tobacco products or nicotine delivery systems (e.g., e-cigarettes) than out right quitting. Also, the cigarette industry gets support for its concerns from the pharmaceutical industry that makes smoking cessation drugs. They too see competition from these safer tobacco products and nicotine delivery systems for their products. They want these competing products stopped and have informally allied themselves with the tobacco and anti-tobacco groups. Because, the one thing all cartels and monopolies have to worry about is some out-of-the-blue entrepreneur coming up with some new unforeseen product, eliminating much of the market for existing products and firms.

Modified Risk cigarettes (the ones that were labeled "low", "mild" "light") can be introduced only if they have scientific evidence showing: 1) the difficult, expensive and time consuming one—that there is a reduced health risk from smoking this brand. This would take a major long-term scientific study going on maybe for 20 years or so. The less burdensome option is the one that allows you to claim that your brand has reduced levels, or is free of a particular harmful substance. For instance, Clarkettes contains less hydrogen cyanide than an average of the top three brands. If you can demonstrate this to the FDA's satisfaction, you may be able to market your new "reduced risk" brand. Then again, maybe not.

According to the ACT," … a modified risk product may be commercially marketed only if the Secretary determines that the applicant has demonstrated that such product, as it is actually used by consumers, will, among other requirements, benefit the health of the population as a whole taking into account both users of tobacco products and persons who do not currently use tobacco products."[25] As they say, the devil is in the details. So what does the "health of the population mean?" There are a number of marketing conditions the FDA must consider before approving any new cigarettes for sale. Among others, they are:

> a) the increased or decreased likelihood that existing users of tobacco products who would otherwise stop using such products will switch to the tobacco product that is the subject of the application; b) the increased or decreased likelihood that persons who do not use tobacco products will start using the tobacco product that is the subject of the application; [and] c) the risks and benefits to persons from the use of the tobacco product that is the subject of the

[24] Health, National Institutes of. September 5, 2006. http://consenus.nih.gov (accessed October 29, 2007).

[25] Family Smoking Prevention and Tobacco Control Act, Pub.L. 111–31, June 2009 H.R. 1256. n.d.

> application as compared to the use of products for smoking cessation approved under chapter V to treat nicotine dependence...[26]

This means if your product causes smokers to switch to your "safe" brand rather than quitting, it cannot be sold. If your "safe" brand causes people to start to smoke, it cannot be sold. If your "safe" brand causes people to use your product to smoke instead of buying traditional smoking cessation aids to reduced their nicotine dependence, it cannot be sold. This last one is designed to keep Big Pharmacy happy; they do not want to lose sales of nicotine gum and patches etc..

These marketing conditions will make it impossible for e-cigarettes and other safe or safer smoking products to be marketed. For instance, in the case of e-cigarettes even if they are proved to be 100% safe, it will be argued that smokers will just switch from a more dangerous brand to the safer brand rather than quitting, so e-cigarettes should not be allowed on the market. Or, if it maybe likely that people who have stopped smoking or new smokers may think of trying the new safer (e-cigarette) product, it cannot be marketed. And finally, if it maybe likely that people who may stop trying to quit smoking via nicotine gum etc.; but instead switch to e-cigarettes or use them, rather than nicotine gum to stop smoking, it cannot be sold. This last proviso is aimed squarely at e-cigarettes. That is why if the FDA gains regulatory authority over e-cigarettes. You will never see an e-cigarette again. The FDA and its client the Big Three cigarette companies will see to this.

All the above will make sure cigarette demand stays inelastic (not very price sensitive); and, since cigarettes and smoking are not a major growth industry, most of the cigarette companies' future revenue growth will come from price increases. Most companies can make more money from raising prices than from increases in unit sales. One economist has estimated that a company with 8.6% tax rate would have to increase unit sales by 4% to get the same profit effect as a 1% increase in prices.[27]

So, what should you look forward to? The FDA will see to it the Big Three cigarette makers continue to make large profits under the government sponsored and FDA administrated cigarette cartel—even OPEC does not have it this good. More dangerous smoking products will be allowed to be sold (grandfathered); new and/or safer products will be prohibited or have their introduction substantially delayed; and, people will be required to continue to smoke more dangerous tobacco products into the distant future. This is why the ACT and the FDA have been called "The Marlboro Monopoly and Protection Act."

On a final note, if the cigarette companies ever tried to do on their own only a fraction of what they are required to do now by law—form a successful

[26] Ibid.

[27] See Roger Briner, "Pricing: The Neglected Orphan," Parthenon Perspectives.

impenetrable cigarette cartel—the whole industry and every cigarette company executive would be charged with a host of both civil and criminal violations of a number of federal and state antitrust laws and statutes. The cigarette companies would probably be fined out of existence, broken up and their executives given long prison sentences. Thanks "do gooders".

Chapter 15

The Greatest Antitrust Buster Ever

Back in late 1990s and early 2000s, while the U.S. Department of Justice's, Antitrust Division was busy trying to break up non-monopoly Microsoft for being a monopoly. The real antitrust work and improvement in consumer welfare was being carried out by, primarily, a freshman at Boston's Northeastern University. This entrepreneur would make a sizable dent in the music recording industry, change how music was distributed, and improved consumer welfare to the tune of billions of dollars per year. This entrepreneur along with his partner probably did more to improve consumer welfare in a year a two than the U.S. Justice Department's Antitrust Division has done since its formation.

The story starts in early 1999; you have decided that you want to expand your music collection. While the internet existed, getting music off the internet was tricky and unreliable. People would spend hours trying to find and pull a song of the internet only to have it fail, fail again and again.

Most likely, you would make a trip to the record store or nearest megastore to purchase a CD (compact disk) album. But first, you had to wait for the store to open, drive, at best, 20 minutes to the record store, park, 10 minutes to find the album and song and pay for it and drive back. Close to an hour of time. How about the weather? Do you go, if it is cold, hot, raining, snowing? Of course, after getting there, you could not just buy a song, since finding and buying a single song was difficult. Most songs were bundled with, let's say, 11 other songs into something called an album selling for $15.00. These other songs may not have done anything for you, but you were required to purchase them as a condition to get the one song you liked. It was pricey too—$15 to get one song!

Of course, you may not be able to find the CD you wanted because they were not properly sorted in the CD bin; or the record store may not have it in stock. No worries; they will special order it for you, spend another 10 minutes filling out the forms and paying for it—there may be an extra charge for the special order—then wait days and weeks for the song or album to come in; then, repeat the trip to the record store.

Look at all the time, money, and aggravation to acquire just one song. Now and then, a trip to the record store was a fun way to browse and kill a couple of hours but not every time[28]. By the way, whatever happened to all those record stores?

28 There were a few other options to get music, for instance, from mail

Meanwhile, back in Boston, some guy named Shawn Fanning was trying find an easier way for people to get together and share their music besides physically exchanging the CDs, or its predecessor, the cassette tape or LPs. Fanning was developing software to make searching for and downloading music files easy and reliable. The software would allow people to dip into each other's hard drives, and share their MP3 music files[29]. The software was very popular. This lead Shawn Fanning and Sean Parker to co-found Napster. What Napster did was: 1) provide a "no charge", downloadable program that transformed PCs into servers for exchanging MP3 music files over the internet by letting individuals tap into each other's music collection; 2) identify any song the user was willing to share with others; and 3) Napster provided a website where that information was made public so person could find the song/album and download it.

The legacy Napster has, mostly courtesy of the Record Industry Association of America (RIAA)[30], was it allowed people to steal music from the rightful owners without having to pay for it. No, this was not the contribution Napster made to society and consumers. It introduced competition to the cartel-like music industry. Napster introduced variety, convenience, reduced record (song) prices, and transaction costs enormously and permanently, something the pre-Napster music industry did not do.

Here is how. The first thing Napster did was provide a massive online library of songs, shortly after its launch in May 1999 as a beta, and by October 1999 it had already 4 million songs. The first thing a user would see would be a massive collection of songs. More songs than you would see in a music store of the day and different versions of the same song, studio, live, acoustic, or covered. Not only was Napster's catalog large and well organized. It was easily searchable via its search engine. You could find almost any song or album instantly. Not only could consumers search current hits, they could easily "backlist mine" or search long forgotten albums, groups, singers, songs, that they liked but had forgotten about, instantly. These artists and albums would have remained undiscovered or forgotten if not for the ease of searching and the linking of titles, artists, and albums together electronically via Napster. (This search tool used in its legal version eventually boosted download sales from backlisted albums and artists.) Try doing this in a traditional record store!

How big and good was Napster's library and search engine? In order to demonstrate Napster's music library prowess and sophistication of its search engine, Napster's nemesis, the RIAA had its member executives play a game that was informally called "Stump the Napster". Executives were challenged to

---

order catalogs.

[29] The MP3 format, devised in the mid-1990s, had become the dominant format for digital audio for the internet age.

[30] Henceforth, called the RIAA. The RIAA is a trade group made up of record companies.

try to find at least one of their company's new songs—released or unreleased—that was not being shared online. They could not.

Napster was convenient. Napster was open 24 hours a day; 7 days a week and 365 days a year. From the convenience of your home and within minutes, you could search, find, download and be listening to your favorite song in minutes, verses an hour long trip to the record store. Napster saved, consumers time and money and provided instant gratification of their music cravings.

Now for the pièce de résistance, the real benefit Napster introduced was a lá cárte song purchases—okay, at first, "no charge" downloads. Before Napster, songs were primarily available or sold in bundles as a collection in a CD. Bundling is one-technique firms with monopoly or some substantial pricing power use to make more money. You do not allow the single purchase of an item; to get one item, you must buy several items jointly. This is what really made music recording and publishing profitable. The company would sign an artist/group to a record contract. Hopefully, the group would come up with one hit song, the record company could put it on an album with 11 other lousy songs and sell it $15.00, so you were in effect paying $15 for a song you liked. It was bundling that made the music industry really profitable.

But, now Napster developed a way to distribute unbundle music. Individual songs were available to be downloaded—there goes the industry's monopoly profits from bundling. Even today artists and record label executives disguise their disgust with lower profits by stating that their songs belong together in an album, and say, "You cannot fully appreciate the music unless you buy and listen to the entire album. It's about the music." You say, "No, it's about the money."

Unbundle songs for sale: this is one genie that the RIAA and its members wish they could get back in the bottle.

These were just a few of the benefits Napster bestowed on consumers.

However, all good things have to come to end, and so it is with the original Napster. Napster was launched in May 1999 and by October 1999, it had 4 million songs in circulation; by March 2000, the Napster community numbered more than 20 million. As many as 57 million people were using Napster at its peak. By the summer of 2000, Napster users were downloading about 14,000 songs every minute. While album sales had been growing over the 1993 to 1999 period by 10% per year, they suddenly dropped by 16% from 1999 to 2000, followed by another 25% from 2000 to 2001. The music industry was horrified and looked to music piracy in general and Napster in particular.

Lawsuits were filed against Napster for breach of copyright. First by A&M Records, Inc. in A&M Records, Inc. v. Napster, Inc. 239 F.3d 1004 [9th Cir. 2001] and then the RIAA sued, so did Metallica and Dr. Dre. The music industry even tried to reduce the demand for illegally unbundled and downloaded music by suing the users themselves. The RIAA and others were claiming music revenues were down because of piracy.

Napster lost. By February 2001, Napster had been ordered to start charging for music downloads or else close entirely. It closed. Interestingly, not a single MP3 was ever stored on its servers; the software simply enabled users to download from each other. This was the electronic equivalent of friends allowing friends to borrow their CDs, tapes, or LPs as done for decades before.

While Napster was finished in its current form, its innovations and consumer savings were here to stay. The question was how to make it legally acceptable to the music industry and profitable for everyone else? This is something the early entrants found to be difficult. In 2001, three major labels—Warner, Bertelsmann and EMI started MusicNet. For $9.95 per month, you could download 100 songs to your computer from a library of 75,000 songs but not burn them to a CD; and the songs would vaporize after 30 days; so, consumers were basically renting songs. In 2001 PressPlay, a venture of Sony and Universal, had a service where you could have 50 downloads and 500 streams per year; and by 2002, PressPlay offered unlimited downloads for $179.40 year. While the music industry was recognizing the desirability of digital music, their legal version came with too many strings, and while Napster was gone, consumers could turn to other peer-to-peer (P2P) web sites such as Kazaa and Grokster.

The next to give it a go was Apple. While Apple announced iTunes in January 2001, it worked only with Apple computers, even the first iPods—available in late 2001—could not help sales. It took until April/May 2003 when Apple delivered its 3rd generation of iPods fully compatible with PCs and brought back a lá cárte pricing to iTunes with pricing of $0.99 per song that things really took off. By 2003, Apple sold its 1 millionth iPod; and, by September 2003, iTunes passed the 10 millionth song mark. By September 2003, Universal was forced to cut the list price of its music by 30%. Now, iTunes is responsible for 70% of legal music downloads. Of course, all of Apple's early music came with those dreaded DRM (Digital Rights Management) restrictions that the record labels required, making sure that consumers could do very little with the songs except listen to them on a certain device.

The next big change was when Amazon Music, launched as Amazon MP3 in the US in September 2007, began selling music downloads exclusively in MP3 format without DRM. Amazon MP3 was the first online service offering DRM-free music from all four major record companies—EMI, Universal, Warner Brothers Records, and Sony Music. ITunes followed.

Shawn Fanning and Napster had changed the music forever, something the RIAA does not like and never let's go of. Today you cannot visit the RIAA's web site and read something about music without seeing the words piracy, losses, and Napster. Usually, all three are put together in the same sentence. Despite the fact the Napster, by 2013, had created a $4.4 billion digital download industry. The RIAA still insists that the reason music sales have dropped by 53% since the advent of P2P sites 15 years ago is because of piracy. No. It is because music prices have dropped from effectively $15 per song (album buying) in 1999 to between $0.69 and a $1.29 per song today.[31] When given a given a choice of buying the entire album to obtain a song, the consumer wants or just a song, consumers choose the song over the album by a 9 to 1 ratio.

Did you ever wonder why songs generally cost between $0.69 and $1.29 per song? It reflects the potential competition from P2P websites. The music industry would like to charge a whole lot more for a song; but they know if they did, consumers would flock back to those pesky little P2P websites and fill up on "no charge" songs. As I said, consumers will pay between $0.69 and $1.29 per song for a legal copy of a song, but not much more. The only decision the music industry and artists have to make is whether they can record and sell music profitably at that those prices. If not, they need to put their high school degrees to work and seek higher paying employment elsewhere.

How about piracy? It had to affect sales. First, the piracy of music, copyright infringement and everything else existed well before Napster. For instance, with cassette tapes, friends would let friends make a tape copy of their album. In fact, the music industry thought CDs would end piracy once and for all given the initial cost of burning a CD. Wrong! Also, flea markets are and have always been an outlet for bootlegged goods, especially in the pre-P2P music days.

Furthermore, despite what you may think, a stolen song does not reduce legal sales by one song. A stolen song may reduce the sales of a paid song only by between a $^{1}/_{6}$ and $^{1}/_{3}$ of song.[32] Illegal music is not a perfect substitute for legal music. For instance, legal digital music would come straight from the music label's master recording. It should be of high fidelity, clear, crisp with no corruptions. P2P music, well, you get what you pay for, sometimes with static, maybe with a mechanical blip and/or computer viruses thrown in. So, people will pay a positive price for legally downloaded music to avoid these issues; plus, it may make them feel better and eliminate the small risk of being caught with an illegal copy.

Another reason most "no charge" music downloads offset legal sales by less than a one to one ratio is because illegal downloads are low valuation music. The consumer would not have purchased the song in the first place. Here is why. If a song sells for a $1.00, only consumers who value the song for

[31] It is the low price of songs, along with "no charge" music downloads that has allowed many college students to mass a music library that would make any pre-2000 radio station envious.

[32] Joel Waldfogell, "Musics Files Sharing and Sales Displacement in the ITunes Era." Philadelphia, June 15, 2009. 2.

a $1.00 or more will purchase it. If a consumer values the song for only $0.50, they will not purchase it at a price of a $1.00. Now, if the consumer downloads a low value $0.50 song from a P2P website at "no charge", the music recording industry suffered no revenue loss (because the consumer would not have purchased it for a $1.00); but, the consumer received a full $0.50 worth of consumer surplus or welfare. There is no loss of revenue to the industry but a gain for consumers and society.[33,34] There was a net societal gain for this transaction.

So, the next time you download a song or album thank Shawn Fanning and his trustbusting effort for affording you this option and for saving you the additional $14 or so dollars.

Napster and P2P websites trustbusting and promoting consumer welfare since 1999.

[33] Of, course, eventually the total revenue the artist receives from any song must be enough for the artist to continue to produce songs.

[34] An illegal download may stimulate the sales of legal music, as they may be a complement to legal music. People who make illegal downloads buy a lot of legal music as well. For instance, people may sample a few unknown songs illegally, like them and decide to purchase some legal songs from the artist.

Chapter 16

Why You Get Paid What You Get Paid

Any resource, including your labor, is not demanded or employed for its own sake, but for the value in creating useful societal products and services. The demand for any resource depends on: 1) how productive the resource is or how much it physically produces or creates; and, 2) how valuable or how much people will pay for the final product. In short, the more productive the resources the more valuable it is. The more valuable or the higher the price of the final product produced with the resource; the more valuable the resource is i.e.; the more people will pay for the resource. The converse is also true, the less productive the resource, the less valuable the final product used to produce the item, the less the demand for the resource and the less will be paid for the resource.

What this means to you dear worker is, you are paid according to how much work you do. Your marginal productivity (MP or your productivity or your productivity at the margin) and how valuable your work is as determined by the price of final product or service sold. Together this is known as your MRP (marginal revenue product) or VMP (value of the marginal product). For instance, a firm only employs a resource if it expects it can make money off it. A firm will hire a worker at $8.00 per hour only if it thinks it can make at least $8.00 per hour in revenues or profits from this worker. If a worker costs the firm $8.00 per hour and the worker generates $9.00 per hour in revenues, it will be hired. The firm will keep hiring workers until the last worker hired, generates in revenue exactly what it costs in wages. In my little example, a firm will hire workers until the revenue generated by the last worker's MRP or VMP is $8.00 per hour and the wage is $8.00.

In case you are wondering how the firm makes its money? It makes it off the inframarginal workers, i.e., the worker who produces $9.00 an hour in revenue but costs the firm just $8 per hour. The firm keeps hiring resources until the MRP declines to $8 per hour (because of diminishing marginal returns); then it stops making money; and, then, it stops hiring. In short, your MRP or VMP on the demand side together with how unique or scarce your skills are on the supply side determine your pay.

Here is what does not determine your pay. You are not paid according to your marital status, the number of children you have, the number of problems you have, how many bills you have, how screwed up your life is, how many bad decisions you have made, or how much you think you deserve or want.

Furthermore, you cannot make more money or generate a higher income, through government legislation, attempting to vote yourself more money, through protests or marches. Some people, probably many misguided people, think that society can legislate a higher standard of living for themselves and others through minimum wages laws. If people will just vote for a higher minimum wage for everyone, everyone will automatically get more money. Look how easy it is. This should tell you it is not.

Many would like to imagine and wish the above were true. Just imagine every person and country in the world could become rich by just having their national or state legislature change a few words of their laws and raise their minimum wage to higher and higher levels. Want more money: Try a hundred dollars per hour how about a thousand dollars an hour? Too bad, it does not work this way. If it did a country like Haiti or the countries of Africa could, legislate their way to riches, by raising their minimum wage. Unfortunately, all this will do is further impoverishing their citizens.

For instance, in my example, if the government comes along and says that the all workers must be paid $9.00 per hour, the last worker that was hired at $8.00 hired will lose a job as the revenue is $8.00 and the wage is $9.00 per hour. The firm will lose money ($1.00 per hour) unless something is done to boost the worker's productivity or MRP to at least $9 per hour.

While, the "do gooders" thought they were helping worker, they just caused a worker to lose a job and a source of income. In short, if a worker is getting a paycheck, it is a market wage not a government wage that is responsible. What does the minimum wage do? It gets people fired or prevents them from being hired, especially the low skill or unskilled workers who it was designed to help. Ever wonder why the teenage unemployment rate in the U.S. 18% and rising? (In some states, it is much higher.) Now you know. Minimum wage laws get the low skilled workers' hours reduced to just the most profitable times and hours for the firm. The result a worker ends up with a smaller paycheck (fewer hours) or no paycheck.

If you want more money, you must increase your MP or marginal productivity; or, make yourself more productive; do more work and have your work product be incorporated in a more valuable product or service. This is the purpose of education. By increasing your education, you are attempting to make yourself more productive and produce more valuable products or services, which can be sold for a higher price. This is the only way you can get more money or a higher income.

Finally, if you do not like the working conditions or pay at your current company, you need to start evaluating your alternatives. Maybe another company will value your skill set more. If they do, then leave your current company. In fact, you have an obligation to yourself, your family, and society, to evaluate your alternatives regularly to make sure that, as a resource, you are allocating yourself to your highest and best use. If you do that, you will benefit by receiving a larger paycheck. If you cannot find a company willing to pay more for your services, then you may have to accept the fact that you are receiving your MRP and are being fairly paid.

Chapter 17

CEOs and Life in the Fast Lane

Every time this topic comes up the discussion gets hot and heavy and I am just thankful that I am not a CEO and my students are not my employees. I mean it is like "Viva la revolución".

First, I generally notice that people make a dichotomy between entrepreneurial CEOs (Chief Executive Officer) and non-entrepreneurial CEOs, i.e., a CEO who becomes a CEO as result of starting his/her own company, such as, Elon Musk, Bill Gates, Oprah Winfrey, Steven Jobs and Mark Zuckerberg and people who just get hired to be CEO of a company. I have noticed people and students are kinder, more tolerate of entrepreneurial CEOs than non-entrepreneurial CEOs.

But, all CEOs have a unique talent. There are not many people that have the skill set necessary to manage and run a large organization, keep it running and most of the time and make correct decisions about what the corporation should do or what investments it needs to make. While a lowly worker can affect corporate profits by a couple of dollars by messing up an order of french fries, the CEO has to make regular decisions worth millions, tens of millions, hundreds of millions, if not billions of dollars. They make the correct decision most of the time. They must be able to handle the fallout if he/she is wrong. Not too many people can do this. If there were, then everyone would qualify for being a CEO. That is why CEOs are scarce resources and command high salaries. Their marginal revenue product (MRP) is very high and not too many people have their skill set. For instance, just look at Mark Zuckerberg and the initial problems Facebook faced. While Zuckerberg may have been a "cool hipster dressed in a hoodie," it does not imply he has the skill set necessary to manage a multibillion-dollar corporation successfully.

CEOs work long hours, usually around eighty-hours a week. They are never off-duty. Even while they are taking a break and spending time in Naples Florida, they are on duty making connections, handling emergencies, thinking about and solving corporate problems and issues. How many lowly workers spend their off time thinking and solving their company's problems and handling emergencies while not working and on vacation?

Now a day, it is fashionable to bash and hate CEOs, at least in the U.S.A. There are many new federal laws holding CEO's criminally liable for almost anything that happens within the corporation. So, if some accountant sends a falsified financial statement up to the CEO and if the CEO unknowingly acts on it; bingo, the CEO can be held criminally liable.

Now, if you are a young aspiring U.S. Attorney with the Justice Department looking to make a name for yourself, are going to get more publicity for yourself bringing charges against a lowly accountant or the big, bad CEO? Even though you may not be able to get a conviction in court, you still be able to get an indictment against them, have them arrested and "frog marched" and "perp walked" in front of rows of media. This should be good enough to help your career as an attorney, and get a high paying job in the private sector.

While some people say "good", the CEO deserved it. CEOs have another opinion. Being a CEO is voluntary and they have options. They do not have to risk it. They have a great skill set—very marketable for lots of money—-and many have wealth, so they retire, move on to other lines of work. Or, maybe take their skills set and go to work for a foreign corporation where the criminal liability is not as absolute. So, then, you need to ask, who is benefiting and who is being hurt by this attitude and these laws as the CEOs remove their skill set from the market or at least the U.S. market? Or, if they do decide to work for U.S. firms, you can bet they are going to ask for a whole lot more money to face these unpleasant scenarios.

How about the CEOs that get bonuses even though the company lost a lot of money? Just because a company lost money does not mean the CEO did not do his job and worked hard. How about if the economy goes into recession and the company loses money, but the CEO's company loses a lot less money than other companies in their industry do. Maybe, the company was forecasted to lose $50 million this year. The CEO works hard and cuts the loss to just $10 million. He just saved the company $40 million. Does he deserve a bonus? If so, how much? It is up the Board of Directors and stockholders, no one else; it is their money.

Let's turn it around, just imagine your company promised you a bonus, if you worked really hard, did a good job and ran a profitable division at work this year, you did; but the company still lost money (the other company divisions lost money, because their managers did not work as hard as you did). Should you get your bonus?

Then, there is the inevitable compliant that the CEO got a bonus and the company made money, while the company laid off workers and froze their pay. Despite what you hear on TV and elsewhere, or think, a company's purpose is not to employ people, give the workers as much money as they think they and their family deserve, make the workers feel good about themselves, provide their health care insurance and retirements benefits, give them time off for families and vacations, it is to make things including, hopefully a profit. The company's job is to produce a product or service consumers want, in the amount they want, at the lowest possible cost. (This is your job as a worker too.) If they do what consumers want, the company will be rewarded with a profit. So, in the above case, it looks like the company did the right thing for consumers, and they were rewarded.

I could go on, but I will not. But, before I leave you here are some more questions to ponder.

What do you think of a multi-millionaire/billionaire CEO like Oprah Winfrey? What about Hollywood movie stars? If they did not get $25 million, a picture, the movie studio could employ lowlier studio tour guides and more slave-like PAs (personal assistants). Should movie stars be required to return their salary if the movie flops and the movie loses money? How about sports stars? Should they be allowed to have so much money? Should they be paid, if their team lost that day (week)? Should they be able to keep their bonuses if their team had a losing season? What if a player did really well, but the team still lost, should they be paid, get a bonus? Or, should each player's pay and bonus depend on the team's performance and other player's performance?

Chapter 18

The Wasteful Corporate Jet

Many CEOs have access to the corporate jets; why do they need them? First, the corporate jet is not a private jet; it is not a luxurious as a private jet. For instance, while a private jet of a celebrity may have satellite TV a corporate jet will have just a DVD player. Why? Satellite TV and wireless internet is an expensive luxury. It costs between $100,000 and $500,000 to install one on a jet, because the satellite dish must be able to track the satellite while the jet climbs, banks and travels at 500+ miles per hour, which is very complicated and expensive. While a corporate jet may look and feel like the first class section of a commercial airline, it is a bare bone first class section.

Second, the corporate jet is available to save the company money. A CEO makes thousands of dollars per hour. Do you want a guy you are paying thousands of dollars per hour to, to hang around an airport for eight hours because of an airline delay? It is far better to have the lowly employee of whom you are paying just $30 hour to hang around and airport for eight hours because of airline delays. You see not everyone is created equal when it comes to the value of his or her time.

When CEOs travel, they do not travel solo. On business, they will travel, with their assistant, the CFO (Chief Financial Officer), the COO (Chief Operating Officer), maybe their government affairs officer, their public affairs officer and their staff, so it a full load. While flying to their destinations, they are conducting business, confidential business. It most likely is cheaper too. This is exactly what the automobile executives were doing when they were accused of hypocrisy when flying from Detroit to Washington, D.C. to ask for bailouts for the auto industry. (You know what I think of bailouts.). However, they had a legitimate business reason for using corporate jets. Do you think you could hold private and confidential conversations among several people while flying commercial?

The third is flexibility. Imagine a group executives located in Chicago need to examine their Southwest Florida corporate branches. They leave their Chicago HQ after work on Monday. They fly to Naples and check in to a hotel. They hold a Tuesday morning breakfast meeting with regional managers; then, they hop on the corporate jet fly to Atlanta and hold afternoon meeting with the Atlanta Metro mangers. They leave right after the Atlanta meeting, fly to Houston and check in to a hotel. They hold a Wednesday morning meeting with Houston regional managers; then they fly back to Chicago early PM and head to the office to report their findings, all the while compiling their findings and reports enroute. Corporate jets allow high priced people to be more productive (efficient), which is what you want. Do you think you could do all this while flying commercial?

The fourth is location. A number of corporations have plant and offices that are off the beaten path. You cannot fly directly to them; instead, you fly into a city several hundred miles away, and then drive to them. Do you think it would be a wise use of people's time to do this? Or would it be better to fly in a corporate jet to a much closer airport?

Chapter 19

Health Insurance

A number of people rely on their employer to provide their health insurance. How did this happen? After all, people do not rely on their employer to provide their homeowners or automobile insurance.

Well, it started back during World War II. The Federal Government imposed mandatory wage and price controls on the economy. Companies could not legally increase wages to attract workers. They needed a gimmick; so, they started to offer workers that joined their firm a deal. They would pay their and their families health care costs. Hence, the genesis of company provided health insurance/care. Around 1943, the IRS sanctioned this move by allowing companies to deduct the cost of providing health care insurance coverage to their employees and ruling that the value of the health coverage the company provided to their employees was not taxable income to the employee.

This is why it is somewhat cheaper to the employee for the firm to provide health insurance than for the employee to purchase health insurance on their own. The "tax shield" component creates this incentive. Remove one or both parts of the "tax shield" component and the incentive for company provided health insurance disappears. Employees would just receive some extra cash to spend as they see fit, and no one would care if they got health insurance coverage from their employer.

Today companies are really sorry they got into the health insurance business. A company's human resource department spends more time and effort to administer and settle health insurance claims of their employees than anything else. And, no matter how much they do, the employee is still not satisfied. Fortunately, they will have a good opportunity to get rid of this mess once and for all, when the full effects of the new federal health insurance law kicks in—the Affordable Care and Patient Protection Act. Ironically, what some have said was that a law that was supposed to insure that more Americans have health insurance will do more to insure that fewer Americans have health insurance. Here's why.

First all health insurance sold must meet new federal standards, and include all sorts of coverage for questionable items. Remember the purpose of insurance is to protect you from, **FINANCIAL DIASTERS**, not **FINANCIAL INCONVIENCES**. Just imagine how expensive car insurance would be, if automobile insurance was required to pay for oil changes, new tires, tune ups, brakes, new custom paint jobs, timing belts, car washes and waxes etc.. Routine physician visits, medicine, and prescriptions are not supposed to be paid for by insurance. There is only a limited supply of health insurance dollars out there; you want to make sure they go to their most important uses.

Under the new health care law, you must pay for coverages that you may not want, e.g., alcohol and drug treatments. This will cause amount you pay for insurance to increase. The second is the exclusion of preexisting conditions. Normally, health insurance does allow people with preexisting conditions to purchase health insurance, or it excludes coverage for their already existing health conditions—for good reason too. If the insurance companies did cover preexisting conditions, it would not be insurance any more. It would be a medical payments plan where the healthy people are required to pay all the medical bills of the sick. It would be a sucker bet, and the healthy people would quickly drop the coverage, if they could.

Health insurance usually works like this. All the healthy people get together and put their money in a pot. Now, if one of them should happen to get sick the money will be used to pay their medical expenses. Since they are all healthy now, they all have an equal chance of getting sick and requiring some of the money sometime in the future. It is fair. Now, if you allow a person with a preexisting condition to join, on day one, they walk in; pay the monthly dues (premium); and, they immediately proceed to lay claim to all the money in the pot, and walk out leaving no money for anyone else. The healthy people feel they just been had, which they have. They want to drop out of this sucker bet health insurance scheme. Oh yeah, they cannot drop out; by law. I know, let us try to save some money for every one by placing annual and lifetime limits on insurance expenditures for any one person. That way everyone will be assured of having at least some health insurance coverage. Sorry, under the new federal health care law no annual or lifetime caps on coverage. The first person to get really, really sick is entitled to all the insurance company's money.

The pre-existing condition also creates the adverse selection problem. Save money, do not buy health insurance; then, when you get really sick call up, order insurance, the really good stuff, with no deductibles and copays. It will cost a $2,000 a month, but you will just need it for a month or two, until you are discharged from the hospital. Then, you can drop it, until you need it again. You cannot be denied coverage. It becomes a good deal for people; pay $2,000 and get your $60,000 coronary bypass operation paid for. Look, $2,000 gets you $60,000. What a good deal

Both of these cases will cause health insurance premiums to skyrocket in the short run and cause the health insurance industry to collapse in the long run. So no one will have health insurance in the end. When Obamacare started, there were estimates are that the bare bones minimum plans that met federal minimums the "bronze" plan will cost $4,000 per person or $16,000 for a family of four. Companies are not going to want or be able to afford this.

Here is how to get around it. Drop it. Since, companies that fail to provide health insurance will be fined, but the fine is a lot less than the cost of the health insurance (fine $2,000 per employee). Also, drop coverage for all part-time workers, if they have it, the new law says you do not have to cover them. Hire more part time workers (30 hours or less per week). Turn full-time jobs into part time jobs. Reduce employment; firms with fewer than 50 workers are exempt. Get below 50 workers. Outsource as many jobs as possible. Also, drop family coverage. The law say's just the worker, not the worker's family. Give the employee a little extra cash to compensate for the loss of coverage.

Now many workers and families will not have coverage. Many workers will not be able to come up with the $4,000 or 16,000 for a family of four. Now it is tax time. Under the law's, individual mandate, you have to have insurance or you will be fined $695 per family member without insurance or 2.5% of the family's income. Your fine will be collected by the friendly folks at the IRS. Many people will find they cannot afford the health insurance premium and will pay the income tax penalty. They will be poorer and still not be able to afford health insurance. The Federal Government will be richer with more tax revenue. That is why this health care law has been labeled the largest tax increase in U.S. history—its true purpose!

Chapter 20

Supply and Demand

Here is some background. Economics is about allocating scare resources to satisfy as many consumer and societal wants as possible. Since everything is scare, we cannot give everybody all or everything they want. Everything must be rationed. The primary way "things" are rationed is through the **price system—**meaning **prices**. Prices usually work so efficiently, conveniently and equitably, you do not know prices are working to ration goods and services and to incentivize more production of these goods and services.

Prices are determined through the interaction of supply **and** demand. Demand represent the forces of buyers of the good and services. Supply represents the forces of the sellers or the producers of goods and services.

Demand

First, the law of demand. The demand curve or demand schedule for a product is many times represented by a straight line called a demand curve which shows an inverse, negative or indirect relationship between the per unit price (P_u) of the good or service and the quantity demanded per unit of time (Q_t). Price is the boss; it tells quantity what to do. A graph of a demand curve shows as price goes up, quantity demanded goes down; and, as price goes down, quantity demanded goes up. Buyers and consumers like lower prices and hate higher prices. This is an inverse or negative relationship. Why is that so? Three reasons:

The income effect. Everybody knows that amount you can buy, Q_t (quantity per unit of time), is determined by your income and the price of the product or Q_t = Income/price, e.g., \$100/\$5 = 20. If the price goes up (down), quantity demand goes down (up). For instance, if your income stays at \$100 and the price goes to \$10, quantity demanded drops to 10 units. The income effect is an important reason quantity demanded is negatively related to price but not the primary one.

Declining or diminishing marginal utility or usefulness of additional units of the product is a more important reason why the demand curve shows an inverse relationship between price and quantity; or why, it is necessary to offer consumers or buyers a lower price to get them to buy additional quantities. The additional units are not as valuable to consumers as previous units.

Let's say you just returned from being lost in a desert for a day or two and immediately stumble upon the Dr. Clark water stand, he is selling water by the glass. How much would you pay for the first glass of cold mountain spring water? A lot, most likely. How about the second? The third? How about the 20th glass of water? Probably, a lot less. Even through each glass of cold mountain spring water is the identical, your monetary valuation of each glass drops with each glass drunk. This is why you see pizza places advertising first pizza full price, get the second at 50% off. The same with theme parks offering additional days at a reduced rate. Think and thank diminishing marginal utility for this.

The substitution effect. If the price of one item goes up (down), you buy less (more) of it; because, you start to purchase more of a substitute product (a product that is similar to the one that just went up in price.) For instance, with Coke and Pepsi, if the price of Coke goes up, people drink less Coke. Why? They start to drink more Pepsi, because Pepsi is now relatively cheaper than Coke is; and, people who were drinking Coke now switch to Pepsi and vice versa, when Coke lowers its price.

Now you know why price is so important, and why we mention it first when discussing the law of demand. After all, if I ask you, if you want to buy something your response would be, "How much (the price)?"

Important: When just the price changes and nothing else changes, we move up and down the same demand curve. It is called **a change in quantity demand**. When we say as price goes up quantity goes down and vice versa, we make an implicit assumption of "other things constant" or the Latin *ceteris paribus*. If these other factors change, then all bets all off. We do not know what will happen without further investigation.

Some other factors that influences demand

Income (+, sometimes -). Many goods are normal goods. If income goes up (down), demand for the product goes up (down) and more (less) of the product is purchased. If income changes, the whole demand curve will shift. This is called a change in demand. Income up; demand up; income down; demand down.

There are some goods that are called inferior goods. In this case, there is a negative or inverse relationship between income and quantity. For instance, if income goes up, quantity purchased of the product goes down and vice versa. An example, of these types of goods are: used cars, used cloths and lard etc.. In this case, income up; demand down; income down; demand up.

Price of substitutes (+). Substitutes are items that can be interchange with one another. The price of substitutes is complicated, because we are talking about how the price of product A influences the quantity purchased of product B. If the price of a substitute changes, then that will shift the whole demand curve for the substitute product in the same direction. For instance, if Coke raises its price, Coke will see a decrease **in quantity demand.** Pepsi will see **an increase in its demand** or **a shift in its demand curve**. Why? In response to the price hike, people will buy less Coke but more Pepsi. The reverse will happen if Coke lowers its price.

Price of Complements (-). Complements are items that go together; or if you buy one item, you buy another item that goes with it for instance, hotdogs and hotdog buns, or rolls. Like substitutes, the price of complements is complicated, because we are talking about how the price of product A influences the quantity purchased of product B. If the price of a complement changes, then that will shift the whole demand curve for the complementary product in the opposite direction. For instance, if the price of hotdogs goes up, you will see a decrease **in quantity demanded** of hotdogs. Hotdog rolls will see **a decrease in its demand** or **a shift in its demand curve** in a downward direction. Why? In response to the price hike people will buy fewer hotdogs, and therefore, require fewer hotdog rolls. The reverse will happen if hotdog prices are lowered and the same with computers and computer software.

Tastes (+). Tastes reflect what you, the consumer, likes or does not like. If you do not like fish, your demand for fish will be zero. If you like pizza a lot, your demand for pizza will be high. Tastes can also reflect what is in fashion or a fad, e.g. skinny jeans. This part of demand can change quickly and drastically as things go in and out of style rapidly. As a businessperson, changes in taste can quickly and drastically affect the demand for your product, and drive you crazy. One minute you have too little of the product; the next minute you have too much product and cannot give the stuff away. Remember: tastes goes up, demand goes up, and the reverse is true. Also, companies advertise to influence taste and therefore demand. Hopefully an increase in advertising will increase tastes and lead to an increase in demand for its products. Sometimes negative advertising is use to reduce demand, e.g., political advertising, and don't smoke and don't use drugs campaigns.

Price expectations (+). This means **how prices in one-time period (tomorrow)** influences **the quantity purchased in another time period (today)**. Price expectations are complicated, because we are talking about how the price tomorrow of product A influences the quantity purchased of product A today. If the price is expected to go up tomorrow, beat the price increase and buy more today. An expected price increase tomorrow means an increase or shift in demand today to beat the prices increase. A lower expected price tomorrow, means a decrease in demand today—wait for the sale—and an increase in demand tomorrow.

Population or number of Buyers (+). The more people or as the number of buyers increase, so does demand. If the population or the number of buyers goes up, it means an increase and shift in demand. The reverse is true as well. Population down; demand down. The addition of this factor turns demand from an individual demand curve into a market demand curve. You can also use a subset of the population here as well, such as, the number people over 65, children under the age of 12, adults between 18 and 22 years old etc. depending on the product.

These are some general all-purpose factors that influence demand. For specific products and services, additional variables may be included or excluded from the demand function or curve. Just remember if just the price changes, the demand curve stays put and we move up and down the same demand curve. If price stays the same and one of the other factors change, the whole demand curve can change, move, or shift.

Supply

The law of supply is represented by a supply curve which is a schedule showing the amount supplied by producers at different prices. It shows an up sloping, a positive or direct relationship between price per unit (P_u) and quantity per unit of time (Q_t). If price goes up, quantity supplied goes up, and vice versa. This is the seller's side of the supply and demand equation. Sellers like higher prices and hate lower prices. Why is there a positive relationship between price and quantity supplied? Three reasons:

Increasing incremental and marginal costs. This means it costs more to produce more. The cost of producing more output requires that a higher price be offered to producers to cover the additional cost of expanding output. Rising marginal cost are induced by diminishing marginal productivity of the inputs or resources used. Of course, the reverse is true, as output shrinks incremental costs go down.

The profit incentive. As prices rise, to some degree, the firm has a chance to make larger profits. The firm responds to this increased profit opportunity by producing more. More output means the more items you can sell which means more profits and money. If prices drop, the profit potential shrinks and firms reduce output.

The opportunity cost of resources. To expand output you need more resources and inputs. How do you get them? You have to bid them away from their alternative uses How do you do this? By paying more for the resources, than other firms are. For instance, to get their workers to become your workers at your firm, you offer and pay them more money. You get the required resources to expand output, but this increases your costs. So price has to go up to cover the opportunity cost of these resources. And, the reverse is true.

Important: When just the price changes and nothing else changes, we move up and down the same supply curve. It is called **a change in quantity supply**. When we say as price goes up quantity goes up and vice versa, we make an implicit assumption of "other things constant" or the Latin *ceteris paribus*. If these other factors change, then all bets all off. We do not know what will happen without further investigation.

Some other factors that influence supply

The price of inputs (-). If the price of inputs (our ingredients) goes up, given our budget (like the income example in demand), we cannot buy as many inputs or resources. Fewer inputs (ingredients) means less output and therefore a decrease in supply. So the price of the inputs goes up, supply goes down; and if the price of inputs down, supply goes up. This shifting of supply is called a change or shift in supply.

Technology (+). Technology is a process of doing things faster, better and cheaper at least *ex ante.* It is a resource multiplier. As technology (resources) goes up, supply goes up or increases. The supply curve shifts outward or goes higher. Note: technology is a one-way street. It always goes up not down at least *ex ante*, not *ex post.* The reason technology is a one-way street is because people always try to make things faster, better, smaller and cheaper. Negative technology would have a goal of making things slower, worse, bigger and more expensive.

Taxes (-) and Subsides (+). Taxes reduce your budget, so higher taxes, lowers your budget; a smaller budget means fewer resources (inputs) are purchased which means smaller output. A smaller output decreases supply. In short, taxes up, supply down; and taxes down, supply up.

Subsidies are the reverse of taxes. The government gives you money. If subsidies go up, the budget goes up and more resources (inputs) are purchased; more inputs mean more output and therefore, supply goes up and vice versa. The supply curve shifts or changes with either a change in taxes or subsidies.

Price of other goods (-). This is another complicated one as we are talking on how the price of one good, good A, influences the quantity supplied of another good, good B. An example will help. A farmer has only so much land upon which he/she can grow wheat or corn. He/she has on his/her land planted 50% each of corn and wheat. If the price of corn goes up, the farmer will plant more corn and grow more corn which means less wheat is grown So, if the price of corn goes up, the supply of wheat will decrease; hence, the negative sign and vice versa.

Price expectations (-). This is the reverse of price expectations for demand (buyers). Why? Sellers like high prices hate low prices. Again, this means **how prices in one-time period (tomorrow)** influences **the quantity sold in another time period (today)**. Price expectations are complicated, because we are talking about how the price tomorrow of product A influences the quantity sold of product A today. If the price is expected to go up tomorrow, do not sell today; sell tomorrow. An expected price increase tomorrow means a decrease in supply today and an increase in supply curve tomorrow to get the benefit of the price increase tomorrow. A lower expected price tomorrow means an increase in supply today and a decrease in supply tomorrow. Got it?

Number of sellers or firms (+). This is like population in demand. The number of firms or sellers goes up; supply goes up; the number of sellers goes down; supply goes down. The addition of sellers or firms into the supply curve turns the supply curve from an individual firms supply curve into a market supply curve.

These are some general all-purpose factors that influence supply. For specific products and services additional variables may be included or excluded from the supply function or curve. Just remember if just the price changes, the supply curve stays put and we move up and down the same supply curve. If price stays the same and one of the other factors change, then the whole supply curve can change, move or shifts.

Supply and Demand

Remember it is not supply or demand; but supply and demand. Unless you have both supply and demand and know what is happening to each in relationship to one another, you will have no any idea what is happening with prices and quantities.

Market Equilibrium is where supply and demand intersect or crisscross, equilibrium or global happiness is achieved. Why? Both buyer and sellers are happy. Sellers can sell all they want **"at that price";** and buyers can but all they want **"at that price."** Flexible and freely adjustable prices allow this to happen. Prices allow both buyers and sellers to achieve equilibrium where supply equals demand and both sellers and buyers are happy!

A shortage is what happens when the market price is too low. Consumers or demanders like low prices so they try to demand or want a lot of the product. Sellers or suppliers hate low prices, so they do not want to supply a lot of the product at this price. There is a shortage as demand is greater than supply. How is it rectified? Prices start to rise. A rising price incentivizes consumers to reduce their quantity demanded, while a rising price incentivizes sellers to increase their quantity supplied. As prices continue to rise at some point quantity demanded will equal quantity supplied. Equilibrium is reached. The price system attacks the shortage problem from two sides. Both the supply and demand are used to alleviate the shortage.

A surplus is what happens when the market price is too high. Consumers or demanders hate high prices so they demand or want little of the product. Sellers or suppliers like high prices, so they want to supply a lot of the product. There is a surplus as supply is greater than demand. How is it rectified? Prices start to fall. A falling price incentivizes consumers to increase their quantity demanded, while a falling price incentivizes sellers to reduce their quantity supplied. As prices continue to fall, at some point, quantity demanded will equal quantity supplied. Equilibrium is reached. The price system attacks the surplus problem from two sides. Both the supply and demand side is used to alleviate the surplus.

As long as prices can freely rise and fall, you will never have a chronic shortage or surplus of anything!

Price ceilings. A price ceiling is a government imposed maximum price a good or service can be sold for. If the maximum price is set below the equilibrium price, it will create a chronic shortage. This is called **an effective price ceiling**. The shortage cannot be alleviated because prices cannot rise to equate supply and demand. The classic example is of rent controls. Some cities impose an effective ceilings or maximum rents landlords can charge. This will create chronic shortages of rental units.

Price floors. A price floor is a government imposed minimum price a good or service can be sold for. If the minimum price is set above the equilibrium price, it will create a chronic surplus. This is called **an effective price floor**. The surplus cannot be alleviated because prices cannot fall to equate supply and demand. The classical example of this is the minimum wage law. This creates a chronic surplus of labor, affectionately called unemployment, particularly among teenagers and minorities.

References

Baker, Kevin Gauntt. "Agency, Thank You For Regulating: Why Philip Morris's Embrace of FDA Regulations Helps the Company But Harms the Agency;." *Administrative Law Review*, Winter 2009.

Barnett, Thomas O. "Interoperability Between AntiTrust and Intellectual Property." *George Mason University School of Law Symposium Managing Antitrust Issues in a Global Market Place.* Washington, D.C.: U.S. Department of Justice, 2006.

Bastiat, Caude Frédéric. "That Which is Seen and That Which Is Not Seen." *Mises Institute.* November 2, 2009. Retrieved from https://mises.org/library/broken-window.

Boudreaux, Donald J. and Burton W. Folsom, "Microsoft and Standard Oil: radical lessons for antitrust reform." *The Antitrust Bulletin/Fall 1999*, Fall 1999: 555-576.

Briner, Roger. "Pricing: The Neglected Orphan." *Parthenon Perspectives.* n.d.

Brynjolfsson, Erik, Micheal D. Smith and Yu Hu. "Consumer Surplus in the Digital Economy: Estimating the Value of Increased Product Variety at Online Booksellers." *Management Science* 49, no. 11 (November 2003): 1580-1596.

Chapman, John ed.*The Best Plays of 1950-1951, Guys and Dolls,* by Damon Runyon. New York: Dodd, Mead and Company, 1951.

Clark, Lawrence. *Tales from the BizarreSide: What Really Happens When Casino Gambling Comes to Town.* Winter Haven, Florida: Clark Economics, 2013.

Clotfeter, Charles T. and Phillip J. Cook, "On the Economics of State Lotteries." *Journal of Economic Perspectives* 4 (Fall 1990): 105-119.

Family Smoking Prevention and Tobacco Control Act, Pub.L. 111–31, June 2009 H.R. 1256.

Fox News. "Study: 'Cash for Clunkers' an even bigger lemon than thought". *FoxNews.com.* August 11, 2014. Retrieved from http://www.foxnews.com/politics/2014/08/11/texas-am-study-cas-for-clunkers-even-bigger-lemon-than-thought

Godshall, William T. MPH. "*E-Cigarettes Politics.*" September 20, 2004. Retrieved from http://www.ecigarette-politics.com/fda-approves-44-cigarette-brands.html

Guryan, Jonathan and Melissa S. Kearney "Gambling at Lucky Stores: Empirical Evidence from State Lottery Sales." *American Economic Review* 98, no. 1 (2008): 458-473.

Hamilton, James L. "The Demand for Cigarettes: Advertising, the Health Scare, and the Cigarette Advertising Ban." *Review of Economics and Statistics*, 1972: 401-411.

Health, National Institutes of. September 5, 2006. Retrieved from http://consenus.nih.gov

Johnson, Peter. "Pornography Drives Technology: Why Not to Censor the Internet." *Federal Communications Law Journal* 49, no. 1 (November 1996): 217-226.

Knight, Brian and Nathan Schiff "Spatial Competition and Cross Border Shopping Eviidence from State Lotteries." *American Economic Journal: Economic Policy* 4, no. 4 (2012): 199-229.

Lichtman, Landes and William Douglas. "Indirect liability fro Copyright Infringement: Napster and Beyond." *Journal of Economic Perspectives* 17, no. 2 (Spring 2003): 113-124.

Mian, Atif and Amir, Sufi, "The Effects of Fiscal Stimulus: Evidence from the 2009 'Cash for Clunkers' Program." *NBER Working Paper Series*, September 2010.

Rob, Rafael and Joel. Waldfogal, "Priacy on the High C's: Music Downloading, Sales Displacement, and Social Welfare in a Sample of College Students." *NBER Working Paper Series*, October 2004.

Satel, Sally L. M.D. "Will the FDA Kill Off E-Cigs." *New York Times*. January 18, 2015. http://nyti.ms/1axlOxp (accessed June 18, 2015).

Taylor, Charles R. and Michael L. Capella, "Smokeless Tobacco Products as a Harm Reduction Mechanism: A Research Agenda." *Journal of Public Policy & Marketing*, Fall 2008: 187-196.

U.S. Food and Drug Administration. "Smokeless Tobacco Product Warning Labels." *Protecting and Promoting Your Health*. n.d. Retrieved from http://www.fda.gov/TobaccoProducts/Labeling/SmokelessLabels/default.htm

Waldfogell, Joel. "Musics File Sharing and Sales Displacement in the iTunes Era." Philadelphia, June 15, 2009.

CPSIA information can be obtained
at www.ICGtesting.com
Printed in the USA
FFOW01n0649160118
44581217-44432FF

9 780996 628709